# THE GOLDEN RUN

## — HENRY DAMANT —

*A nostalgic memoir of the halcyon days of the Great Liners
to South and East Africa*

**RMS Windsor Castle**

print
matters

*The Golden Run*
*A nostalgic memoir of the halcyon days of the Great Liners to South and East Africa*

Copyright © 2005 by Henry Damant

First Published in South Africa in 2006

Published by Publishing Print Matters (Pty) Ltd
P O Box 44926, Claremont 7735, Cape Town, South Africa

www.printmatters.co.za

ISBN: 0-620-35030-X

Design & Management: Stuart-Clark & Associates cc, Cape Town
Editing: Hazel Petrig and Mark Muller
Digital Formatting: The Design Drawer cc, Johannesburg
Scanning: Castle Graphics (Pty) Ltd, Cape Town
Printed and bound by Creda Communications (Pty) Ltd, Cape Town.

Front Cover: **Windsor Castle** *farewell.* South African Airways
Back Cover: **Windsor Castle** *leaving Cape Town.*

PLEASE NOTE
*The majority of the photographs, publicity material and press cuttings reproduced in this memoir form part of*
*my private collection of such memorabilia collected over the last seventy years.*
*Whilst every effort has been made to acknowledge the sources of this material,*
*regretfully sources of some images have proved impossible to trace.*
Henry Damant

# Contents

# FOLDER MAP OF

## AFRICA

*THE*

*GOING'S GOOD*

*BY*

## UNION-CASTLE

See inside back cover: **Union Castle map of Africa**

# INTRODUCTION

The Union-Castle Mail Steamship Company was a giant among ocean-going shipping lines. It all started in 1853 when the Union Steamship Line was founded and four years later secured the first contract for a regular mail service between the Cape and England, which it maintained for the next fifteen years.

In 1872 the legendary Sir Donald Currie, a major sponsor of South African sport and the building of the Mount Nelson Hotel, founded the Castle Steamship Company. A saga of great rivalry and cut-throat competition between the two shipping companies followed, each trying to outdo the other by building ever-larger mail-ships and sailing ever-faster to the Cape. Over the next eighteen years the voyage time was cut from twenty-three days to a remarkable fourteen days, eighteen hours and fifty-seven minutes by the Union Line's *Scot* – a record held for more than forty years, until broken by the Union-Castle's *Stirling Castle* on her maiden voyage in 1938. In 1900 the two Lines amalgamated to form the famous Union-Castle Line to operate the mailship contract in peace and war for the next seventy-seven years.

Union-Castle – and latterly Safmarine – played an enormous part in the development of South Africa. Certainly, South Africa owes the two companies a considerable debt of gratitude for opening up and maintaining communication and trade links during their lifespan.

Some twenty years after the final mailship sailed from Southampton, passengers aboard the Fred. Olsen cruise ship, *Black Watch*, bound for the Cape, packed the ship's cinema and its aisles to hear my version of the Union Castle/Safmarine story: what follows is that story.

## LIFE ON BOARD OVER 90 YEARS AGO

My mother (far right) on board *RMS Grantully Castle* (7 617 tonnes) on her maiden voyage to the Cape in 1910. Four years later, following the outbreak of the First World War *Grantully Castle* was converted into a hospital ship and remained so until the cessation of hostilities, when she was refurbished and continued on the Golden Run.

## PRELUDE

# LIFE IN THE CITY IN THE THIRTIES

In the mid thirties the Union-Castle Steamship Co. Ltd boasted a fleet of ten mailships on the famous Cape run, ten liners on their "Round Africa" service, six refrigerated cargo vessels for Cape Fruit and six general freight carriers.

It is at this stage that my story begins, for on 29 October 1935 I joined the Union-Castle Line as a junior clerk at the company's Head Office at 3 Fenchurch Street in the City of London. So began my long association with South Africa.

A tall building on the corner of Gracechurch Street, 3 Fenchurch Street housed the Company's various departments on five floors, which were reached either by stairs or an antiquated lift operated by Charlie, the liftman. There was no central heating, each department being warmed in winter by an open coal fire, nearest to which sat the departmental head, while the most junior employee was charged with the responsibility of keeping the fire going, the buckets of coal being replenished by a uniformed messenger boy.

It is interesting to record that I was interviewed for this, my first job, at 10 am on a Monday and at 4 pm that same afternoon received a letter at home confirming my appointment as junior clerk and instructing me to report to Head Office the next morning. After all these years the Post Office, good as it is in many ways, just could not match that today.

It was a time when jobs were for life, and employment in companies such as Union-Castle was much sought after. Office hours were from 9.15 am to 5.15 pm and 9.15 am to 1.30 pm on Saturdays. Luncheon was provided free on a daily basis for each member of the staff, the menu consisting of soup, a main course and a pudding. On Saturdays it was cold meat, biscuits and cheese. There were three sittings – at noon, 12.45 and 1.30 pm; this allowed about twenty minutes before returning to one's duties. This short break was frequently spent on nearby Tower Hill, where the attractions ranged from a pretty teenager named Joan Rhodes, who tore telephone books in half with her bare hands, to the Rev. Donald Soper, who stood on a small wall to preach and obviously enjoyed hecklers, to whom he gave as good as he got.

Recent 'dress down' (casual) Fridays in the City are hailed as something new. Not so, for way back in the thirties 'dressing down' was the order of the day for Saturday mornings at Union-Castle. From Mondays to Fridays we wore stiff white collars, a dark suit (maybe even black jacket and waistcoat with striped trousers), a sombre tie and, of course, black shoes. But on Saturdays it was a case of almost anything goes! Sports jackets with the loudest of check patterns, club ties with the brightest stripes, grey flannels,

*Head Office of the Group at 2 & 4 St Mary Avenue, London EC3.*

**7**

The shorthand qualification proved particularly useful when it was reported to management that a certain Music Hall comedian's act consisted of a monologue describing the disgraceful goings-on on board the good ship *Immoral Castle*.

Since there was then a *Balmoral Castle* in the fleet one of the more qualified junior clerks was dispatched to Finsbury Park Empire to record the act verbatim.

In the event no further action was taken, as management apparently felt that those travelling Union-Castle – particularly in First Class – were unlikely to frequent Music Halls.

and either heavy brogue or suede shoes, were chosen by the majority, whilst some favoured plus-fours, those loose knicker-bockers bagging below the knees, then worn for golf.

Known to the seagoing staff as 'Bleak House', 3 Fenchurch Street certainly had a Dickensian quality about it, not the least in some of the staff. And what characters they were. Take, for example Bob Marleton, who was baggage master for the Union-Castle ships sailing from London Docks. One foggy day in November, with trains at a standstill, coaches were hastily laid on to convey passengers to the quayside. Each coach had a member of staff in charge and those in Marleton's coach were regaled in true Cockney fashion throughout the slow journey through the gloom with his pointing out those famous buildings and notable landmarks still just about visible. "And now, ladies and gentlemen," said Marleton, as they travelled ever deeper into dockland, "we come to the most important building of all." As the passengers craned forward to peer through the fog, Marleton pointed to a small terraced house, and announced proudly, "There we are, ladies and gents, the 'ouse where your 'umble was born!"

Junior clerks, on joining, were posted willy-nilly to whichever department had a vacancy and usually there they stayed for the rest of their careers, resulting in many a square peg in a round hole. By the end of

your first two years with the company you were required to be proficient in both shorthand and typing.

Present day management consultants would have had a field day. Modern skills such as marketing, public relations and personnel management were unknown. Progression through the company was a matter of seniority based on years of service. Promotion was gained by filling a dead man's shoes. Since Union-Castle enjoyed a virtual monopoly on the Cape run there was little or no real 'selling' as we see in the travel industry today. Press relations were non existent. The official company policy in that regard could be summed up in two words: "No comment".

The great company, for great it was, had about it a dignity and pride. After all, someone, sometime, had had the flair and imagination to paint the hulls of the majestic Union-Castle liners in unique and distinctive lavender grey.◆

*Union-Castle passenger office.*

## CHAPTER ONE

# TEN DRAMATIC YEARS: 1945 – 1955

### 1945

Union-Castle was fortunate indeed to have Sir Vernon Thomson at the helm during the immediate post-war years. Since the end of the First World War he had played an important part in shipping, culminating during the Second World War in his appointment as principal shipping adviser and controller of commercial shipping at the Ministry of War Transport. Taking over again as chairman and managing director of the Union-Castle Line after the war, he successfully piloted the great shipping company through the difficult years ahead.

*Sir Vernon Thomson.*
*This portrait by the well known artist David Jaggers hung for many years in the Union-Castle boardroom in the city.*

In 1945, with the war in Europe virtually over, the South African Government invited Sir Vernon to fly out and discuss a new mail contract. The magnificent fleet, so carefully built up by Sir Vernon during the pre-war years, had suffered severe losses. Those that had survived were still under government requisition, engaged on trooping and other duties throughout the world. When war broke out in 1939 the Union-Castle fleet consisted of eighteen passenger liners and ten cargo ships, of which no less than thirteen were subsequently lost through enemy action, six being torpedoed and sunk by German U-boats.

He successfully negotiated a ten-year contract for a weekly service to start in January 1947, and capped the arrangements by announcing that two large passenger liners, each of 28 000 tonnes, were to be built by Harland & Wolff in Belfast to replace the *Warwick Castle* and the *Windsor Castle*, both torpedoed and sunk during the war.

While other ship owners were cautiously holding back from rebuilding their fleets – decisions they were later to regret – Sir Vernon had the foresight, coupled with the courage, to go ahead immediately. As early as January 1945, the financial columns in the national press were forecasting the South African route would be the first ocean liner service to be fully restored to pre-war schedules.

### 1946

My somewhat unspectacular career as a junior clerk had been terminated abruptly in mid August 1939, when as a Territorial Army Royal Fusilier, I was called up. Surprisingly, the excuse given was "trouble from the IRA."

I eventually returned to Union-Castle in the spring of 1946. The demand for accommodation was then intense. Not only were many eager to emigrate, but there were also thousands anxious to return home to South Africa, visit relatives or go out on business. Every day the passenger department was besieged by those desperate to secure a sailing.

On one occasion the gorgeous wife of a celebrated South African-born entertainer offered me £50 – the equivalent today of over £1000 – if I obtained them berths. Each sailing day saw thousands lined up on the quayside at Southampton, bags packed and ready to go. Today's equivalent of 'stand-bys' were then known as 'pierhead jumps', ever hopeful of taking advantage of a last minute cancellation.

### 1947

This year was both an eventful and an important one, not only for the Union-Castle line, but also for South Africa.

True to his word, as Sir Vernon Thomson had agreed two years earlier with the South African Government, the mail service resumed on 2 January 1947, with the sailing from Southampton of the vessel *Roxburgh Castle*, built in 1945 to replace the vessel of the same name sunk in 1943.

Then, seven days later, the line's flagship, *Capetown Castle*, first of the passenger mailships to be reconditioned to pre-war standards, sailed for the Cape.

On February 17 the late King George VI and Queen Elizabeth (the late Queen Mother) with their two daughters, the present Queen and the late Princess Margaret arrived at Cape Town in *HMS Vanguard* at the start of their historic visit to South Africa. Their travels in Southern Africa took

## RMMV *Capetown Castle* 1938 –1967

UNION-CASTLE LINE TO SOUTH AND EAST AFRICA.

THE UNION-CASTLE ROYAL MAIL MOTOR VESSEL " CAPETOWN CASTLE."   27,002 TONS.

SOUTH AFRICA had for long asked for a ship to be called *Cape Town Castle*, but their requests were repeatedly turned down on the grounds that the castle was in fact a fort. Eventually it was accepted as a castle, but with the word Cape Town as one word. Nevertheless, the tradition of naming the ships after ancient castles and residences of Britain was broken. Subsequent non-existent castles included Bloemfontein, Kenya, Pretoria, Rhodesia and Transvaal.

Built by Harland & Wolff, Belfast, *Capetown Castle* was launched on 23 September 1938 by Mrs JD Louw, the Mayoress of Cape Town, and left on her maiden voyage on 29 April, as the line's flagship. Accommodation was available for 290 First and 500 Cabin Class passengers.

The largest Union-Castle motor-driven liner, *Capetown Castle* was also the longest (734 feet) motor liner in the world, and heralded a new, sleeker line in future mailships. Converted into a troopship at the start of the war, she came through unscathed, and duly refitted, sailed again for the Cape on 2 January 1947.

From 1965, refitted as a one-class ship, *Capetown Castle* operated and extra sixteen day service to the Cape via Madeira, Ascension, St. Helena and Walvis Bay. In 1967 she was withdrawn from service and put up for sale.

them over four thousand miles, mostly by train and partly by air. This memorable visit terminated when the Royal Family sailed out of Table Bay on 24 April bound for England via St. Helena.

The demand for accommodation had in no way diminished, a situation of which Sir Vernon Thomson was very conscious, particularly as many of those seeking passages were regular pre-war clients. So he had an Air Bookings Section set up, saying, "If we can't get you back by sea, we'll fly you there." The new section was headed up by Leslie Webb, an energetic man with a wide-ranging knowledge of passenger travel. Since my return to the office I had spent an uninspiring period as personal assistant to the then head of the Passenger Department. So I was delighted in March 1947 to be asked to join Leslie as his assistant.

Gradually we found we were not only booking passengers on flights to South Africa, but to the rest of the world as well, making such sea bookings as we could by other lines, booking hotels, car hire, etc. In short, we had become fully fledged travel agents, and were justly proud when BOAC (today's BA - British Airways) informed us we were their biggest agents in the City. This situation was not exactly popular with the travel agents themselves.

Once the accommodation position returned to something approaching normality, Union Castle Travel (as the section became known) remained as a service to the line's passengers for their additional travel requirements, as well as offering facilities world-wide.

Thirty years later the mail and passenger-line services ceased operations, but the

We used all airlines then serving South Africa, including Sabena, the Belgian airline where Mrs Black was in charge of reservations. One day frustrated by my call to her regarding a certain passenger's third change in his plans, she exploded. 'Mr Damant,' she said, 'There are three kinds of people in this world - men, women and passengers!'

travel agency continued to function and in 1997 celebrated its golden jubilee. Of all the facets making up this great shipping empire, just one has survived – Union-Castle Travel in West London.

The two big ships announced by Sir Vernon when he clinched the mail contract two years earlier were duly launched – *Pretoria Castle* on 19 August and *Edinburgh Castle* on 16 October.

Having ensured the future of the mail service, the Chairman then turned his attention to Union-Castle's popular Round Africa service and placed an order with Harland & Wolff for four new ships. They were to be unique in that they were to carry passengers in one class only, a new venture for Union-Castle.

The Round Africa schedule of sailings from the London Docks to South and East Africa was inaugurated in the early 1920s. The service, a nine week voyage, operated twice a month and alternated clockwise via the Suez Canal or anti clockwise via the Cape.

During the pre-war years, when Britain still had her empire, the colonies were administered by Colonial Officers. It was these officials and their families who largely filled the ships on the Round Africa run, especially when taking home leave.

However, the service also offered an opportunity for other passengers to enjoy a round voyage of close on nine thousand miles, with some twenty points of call with such romantic sounding names as Zanzibar, Dar es Salaam and Lourenço Marques plus Mediterranean ports, the Atlantic Islands, and, of course, Cape Town.

It was currently boomtime in South Africa. New goldfields had been discovered, the Rhodesia's (today Zimbabwe and Zambia) were expanding, and there was the ill-fated East Africa groundnut scheme.

Skilled men were urgently needed and in the austerity of post-war Britain many saw their future in sunny South Africa. To encourage this the South African Government sponsored an immigration scheme and looked to Union-Castle to provide the necessary transport. They prevailed upon Sir Vernon, whose policy had always been to support South Africa to the utmost, to delay for twelve months the re-conditioning of three of the mailships – *Carnarvon Castle*, *Winchester Castle*, and *Arundel Castle*.

The accommodation offered was certainly austere, as the vessels were still fitted out as wartime transports, so when *Carnarvon Castle* inaugurated the scheme in June 1947, she carried 1 283 passengers as opposed to her normal complement of 612. She was followed by *Winchester Castle* (877 passengers) and *Arundel Castle* (846 passengers).

During the eventful year of 1947 Sir Vernon invited the thirty-six year old Francis Keenlyside to join Union-Castle's top management team. As Principal Private Secretary to four Ministers of Shipping and Transport during the years 1939-1943 and Assistant Secretary in charge of the Shipping Policy Division from 1943, Keenlyside was well known to Sir Vernon Thomson. It is said the salary the Chairman had to offer to persuade him to join the Company resulted in his fellow executives receiving unexpected rises in order to bring their salaries into line.

He had an impressive record. Educated at Charterhouse and Trinity College, Oxford, Keenlyside had first class honours in Philosophy, Politics and Economics. A Whitehead Travelling Student ,he had entered the administrative class of the Civil Service in 1934. He had married when twenty-four and had four children. If it is true that opposites attract then here was a classic example. Unlike Sir Vernon – Methodist, bachelor, strict teetotaller and a non-smoker – Francis Keenlyside enjoyed wine, women, and song – provided the last came from *Don Giovanni* or *Figaro*.

Fair and slim, with a passion for mountaineering, his sudden appearance in the Passenger Department would cause bewilderment among the Union-Castle diehards. Occasionally he could be ice-cold and aloof – some would say arrogant and rude. Certainly he did not suffer fools gladly. A typical Keenlyside reaction was his response to a memorandum seeking his authority to purchase a further supply of metal signs inscribed "Agent for the Union-Castle Line" as were widely used pre-war affixed to agent's walls. He wrote: "No doubt during the 1890s these signs were the *dernier cri*. Now they shout to the world a tasteless conservatism we would do well to hide"". Some years later he told me he thought they looked like the advertisements for Monkey Brand Soap that used to appear on Railway Stations.

*Francis Keenlyside*

Then there was the case of the docks office clerk who was in financial difficulties. Staff Department set out his financial commitments in a report to Keenlyside, but unfortunately showed the annual amount against rates per month. His memo was returned with the brief comment, "He should move to a smaller palace."

Most of the older members of staff did not quite know what to make of him, but the younger element were quick to realise and appreciate his impact. Not only was he prepared, from time to time, to come down from Olympus and drink with them, but he was also anxious to bring a much-needed train of modern thought into the overall running of Union-Castle.

Keenlyside had, incidentally, joined Union-Castle on the clear understanding from Sir Vernon Thomson that he was the heir apparent.

## 1948

It was around this time that Frederick Ellis, famous City Editor of the Daily Express, coined the phrase, 'The Golden Run'.

Under the headline, 'Golden Run makes Millions', he wrote in May 1948:

> ... among shipping men Sir Vernon has a reputation for being a tough man. He believes more in ships than shareholders. Since 1934 he has spent millions in building up the Union-Castle fleet. His foresight is building up big money now, for his trip to the Cape has become 'The Golden Run'. Two years is the waiting time for a passenger to South Africa. Some three thousand passengers a month go the Union-Castle way, including one thousand immigrants.

Over the years Ellis had developed a love-hate relationship towards Sir Vernon. He would readily admit that Sir Vernon lived for ships and acknowledged his foresight in rebuilding, but could seldom resist mentioning he was teetotal and non-smoking and often described him as "canny" and "tight-fisted" for keeping the dividend down year after year, whatever the profits.

## 1949

"Another bumper year on the Golden Run to the Cape," reported Frederick Ellis, but by now the strain on passenger space was at last beginning to ease.

The Immigration Scheme finished in May 1949 – a year later than originally requested by South Africa – by which time it was estimated that approximately 32 000 people had sailed to their new homes in South Africa by the three civilian transports.

Now, for the first time since the end of the war, ships were leaving Southampton with empty First Class berths. Now, too, with competition from the airlines mounting, it was very necessary for Union-Castle to start selling. One obvious medium through which to increase passenger business was the travel agent. I was, therefore, naturally excited to be told in December 1949 that this was to be my responsibility.

## 1950

Before the war, representatives of major shipping lines – apart from Thomas Cook, Dean & Dawson, Pickfords, and a few other multiple concerns – were only travel agents part time, their principal business being that of, say, estate agents or auctioneers, with travel merely a sideline. This situation applied particularly to South and East Africa, where Union-Castle was represented on an agency basis, mainly by solicitors, estate agents and the like, but after the war the travel scene changed dramatically.

Firstly, owing to complicated health and passport requirements, currency restrictions and other regulations, a booking took far longer to effect. Furthermore it was necessary to keep constantly *au fait* with the latest rules and regulations. This meant that such firms as estate agents had neither the time nor the staff to cope with this extra work and decided to give up the travel side of their business.

Another factor was the entry on the travel scene in a big way of the International Airlines. There had of course been Imperial Airways pre-war, but its set up was nothing compared to the emerging airlines like BOAC, Air France, KLM, Sabena and Pan American, etc. All these airlines set out immediately to curry favour with the travel agents. Indeed, many an agent spent a fortnight's holiday in South Africa as a guest of the airline concerned. In this way they achieved their initial objective of not only establishing the friendliest of relations with the agents, but also of putting air travel well and truly on the map.

Indicative of the then growing importance to the travel trade agent was the formation the following year of the Association of British Travel Agents (ABTA).

It would not be an exaggeration to say that, for the most part, the Union-Castle Passenger Department resented the existence of the travel agent. To pinpoint their objection would be difficult, but frequently they conveyed the impression that the commission paid to the agents came out of their own pockets.

The fact remained that travel agents existed and, what was more, they were growing in importance as far as the whole of the travel trade was concerned. Simply to ignore them would not make them go away. However, if the Company's objections to agents were as strong as they often appeared to be, they should surely have cancelled them and paid no commission. On the other hand, since they continued to recognise them, they should not have done so reluctantly. Rather, they should have given them every assistance through a comprehensive back up service and aimed to have made them tantamount to branch offices of Union-Castle. In this way the Company could enjoy a network of sales points throughout the UK – and indeed world wide.

At the 1953 ABTA convention in Torquay, a delightful touch was contributed by the convention secretary at the shipping session which was held on Thursday afternoon. At 4 pm precisely he stopped the proceedings and addressing our general manager who headed up the Union-Castle delegation, said, "It's four o'clock, Sir. Have I your permission to let the mail-ship sail?" This was greeted with cheers, laughter, and applause.

Now we could truthfully claim that the travel world recognised the unique service the Union-Castle Line offered to South and East Africa. There was also added satisfaction that our bookings through these agents had by then increased by over thirty percent.

Certainly this was the way I proposed approaching my new task. Regular calls on our agents and visits to the ships when in Southampton formed an important part of my overall plan. These activities, coupled with membership of the international travel club Skäl, the City Travel Club, and the Chamber of Commerce for London, plus attendance at the annual ABTA convention, the West End Passenger Agents annual dinner, and the Southampton Press Ball, all played their part in winning friends and influencing people.

## 1951

A religious man, Sir Vernon Thomson staunchly maintained his span of life was the biblical three score years and ten. Any time beyond these years was a bonus from the Almighty. On 10 February 1951 he reached his seventieth birthday. By nature he was a kindly person as the following will show. He must also have been a rather lonely one, living as he did virtually alone at *Hawthornden*, a large house on Hadley Common near Barnet in Hertfordshire.

However, Sir Vernon was fully occupied in the evenings immediately prior to his seventieth birthday. He was signing cheques on his personal account for twenty five guineas for each and every member of his staff. Each cheque was accompanied by a note addressed personally and marked "Private". The note read : "To mark the occasion of my seventieth birthday I would like to make a gift from myself personally (not from the Company) to each member of the staff. Accordingly a cheque for twenty-five guineas is enclosed, which please accept with my best wishes. No acknowledgment is necessary." A colleague described Sir Vernon's action as "A princely gesture." Over half a century ago twenty-five guineas was a "princely sum" indeed.

The climax of the birthday was the Chairman's tea party. All were invited by Sir Vernon to take tea with him one Saturday afternoon on board the latest addition to the fleet, the *Rhodesia Castle* in the London Docks. Tea was on the scale of bygone days, with thin sandwiches, tea cakes and scones, preserves (not jams), and tea in delicate bone china cups. Before sitting down to the feast, everyone was introduced to Sir Vernon and shook hands with him. In front of me in the long line waiting to be received was Jeanne Whitlock, my typist – the title 'secretary' was unknown in those days. She thanked him for the occasion and Sir Vernon bowed to her with old world courtesy, saying, "It's a pleasure, Miss Whitlock." Jeanne talked about it for days.

## 1952

**Kenya Castle 17 041 tons.**

*Kenya Castle*, sister ship to *Rhodesia Castle* and the fifth new passenger liner to be built for Union-Castle since the war entered service in the spring. In his speech at a luncheon to the press on board the new one-class vessel prior to her maiden voyage around Africa, Francis Keenlyside referred to Kenya Castle as "being designed for the new poor who are now the majority of our reputable population." His comment made all the front pages the next day.

**The Union-Castle Line SS Rhodesia Castle – 17 041 tons.**

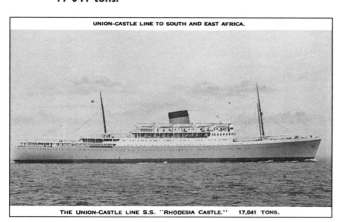

UNION-CASTLE LINE TO SOUTH AND EAST AFRICA.

THE UNION-CASTLE LINE S.S. "RHODESIA CASTLE." 17,041 TONS.

## 1953

On 29 January Sir Vernon Thomson had a heart attack. He was taken to the Middlesex Hospital in London where he died on 8 February two days from his seventy-second birthday. This was little short of tragic, as later that year the Union-Castle Line was to celebrate its hundredth year of existence. To do so without the man who had been at the helm for so many years was a cruel stroke of fate.

But the many fine ships he had built, with their sleek and beautiful lines, like great steam yachts, would for many a year remain as a memorial to his courage and initiative, and also to his abiding love of ships and of the line he had served so well. Sir Vernon left a fleet of twenty-six ships totalling more than 400 000 gross registered tonnes and manned by some five thousand seamen. In his last year one hundred and twenty round voyages were made, fifteen million tonnes of cargo were carried, and more than seven million meals were served to passengers.

Inevitably, Sir Vernon's sudden death posed problems, not least of which was the fact that he had been a virtual dictator, albeit a benevolent one. He had denied his executives any sort of decision-taking. He had taken the decisions, large and small, and had refused to delegate responsibility. Added to which it would be true to say the various departmental heads – they were not given the title of manager – went in some fear of

> **CENTENARY**
> The reason for such a celebration was obscure. Union-Castle as such was only 53 years old, while the regular mail service to South Africa was inaugurated in 1857. So what exactly occurred in 1853 to justify a centenary celebration? In 1853 the Southampton Steamship Company was formed and, later that year, changed its name to the Union Line. Four years later it was to bid successfully for the mail contract to South Africa. So 1953 for Union-Castle centenary was stretching it a bit. But it was Coronation Year, the new mail ship *Pretoria Castle* had been one of the ships at the Royal Fleet Review, and so much had been achieved since the end of the war that a celebration was surely justified.

him. Not surprisingly, for he had a violent temper, as the press had revealed following the 1948 AGM when they described him as being "white with rage as he shouted across the table, which he angrily thumped."

Union-Castle's deputy chairman was Sir George Perrin Christopher, and on 16 February he became the Company's new chairman and managing director. Then sixty-three he was chairman of the Hain Steamship Company and had been director of commercial services at the Ministry of War Transport from 1941 to 1945. He had considerable experience of tramp shipping, but little or none of operating passenger liners.

It would be neither unfair nor unkind to say that Sir George was overawed by his new responsibilities. Commenting on the appointment "Peterborough" wrote in the *Daily Telegraph* the next day: "He will meet heavy pressure from the shareholders to increase dividends. Under the long and beneficent reign of the late Sir Vernon Thomson the company's financial structure became one of the strongest in the city. For years he maintained an exceedingly conservative dividend policy". Two months later Sir George 'celebrated', as the press put it — his first dividend payment in his capacity of chairman by giving the shareholders a rise.

"Changed days," said Frederick Ellis in the *Daily Express*. Just how changed was soon to be seen. In June Sir George was telling shareholders the fleet that had cost £33 million to build would cost £84 million to replace at the then shipyard quotes. He told shipbuilders bluntly that he would order no more ships "at these dizzy prices" (but in under two years he was forced to place an order for a new mailship).

Worse was to come, for only seven months after Sir Vernon's death the city was rife with rumours of take-over bids for Union-Castle. In mid September Sir William Currie, chairman of P & O issued a denial that they were seeking to obtain an interest in Union-Castle. Sir George was quoted as saying, "there is no shadow of truth in it." In early October The Times reported that United Molasses who had bought the Anchor Line four years previously for £3 million, had issued a notice to their stockholders to the effect that "neither the company nor any of its subsidiary or associated companies had made, or intends to make, a bid for the controlling interest in Union-Castle Line."

This wretched situation brought forth a veritable broadside from the *Sunday Express* on 11 October 1953. They wrote: "The centenary of the Union-Castle Line should be a time of rejoicing for the shareholders, yet they rejoice not at all. What a pathetic situation is here. Ten days ago there was fun and games in the market because it was thought that somebody was about to bid £4 a share to get control of Union-Castle's magnificent fleet of liners and cargo ships. Why pathetic? Because £4 represents less than half of the true value of the shares in terms of the ships and the superabundance of cash. The shareholders should not pin their hopes on outside buyers who see in the grand old company a chance of a quick profit of a few million pounds. Sir George has been warned. The red light is aglow in the boardroom. If he wants to avoid an ignominious take-over deal and the end of his long connection with the line he cherishes, he need take only one simple step. By doubling the dividend to a modest fifteen percent he can get his shares up to a price which will warn off the take-over boys, satisfy his shareholders, and increase his own prestige."

In this unhappy atmosphere Sir George announced a dinner and dance at Grosvenor House for staff and their wives (a revolutionary step) to celebrate the "centenary". Dress for the occasion? Dinner jackets or lounge suits we were told. Following discussions in depth at either the *ABC* over coffee or the *Blue Anchor* over a pint, we decided dinner jackets (DJs) would be *de rigeur*, particularly as the ladies would be in evening dress. Then, at the eleventh hour, with an overwhelming majority of the staff committed to a not inconsiderable investment at Moss Bros, the chairman let it be known that he would be wearing a lounge suit.

The great day – or, rather evening – duly came. After an excellent dinner, the chairman spoke. I well recall my wife Linda's horror, not at the speech, but at the gentleman on her left. He, a fairly senior member of the company, was asleep. Even the surprise revelation from Sir George that we all had field-marshall's batons in our knapsacks failed to rouse him. However he came to when a spontaneous burst of applause greeted the chairman's announcement that Keenlyside was to be made general manager.

A member of the staff with appropriate length of service had been delegated to reply. In all fairness a difficult task, but he caused some consternation when he ended his speech by requesting "all the gentlemen to get their ladies on the floor". The less inhibited greeted this exhortation with ribald guffaws of laughter.

I must confess that, on balance, I preferred Sir Vernon's tea party to Sir George's dinner and dance.

## 1954

The death of Sir Vernon had been the cue for every departmental head to re-submit to the new chairman their pet schemes which, over the years, had been turned down. Sir George agreed to many of the plans put forward and even gave the shareholders a rise.

Finally he succumbed – at last – to ever-increasing pressure to build a new liner for the mail service. Early the next year an order was placed with the company's regular shipbuilders, Harland & Wolff in Belfast, for a new mailship.

He had given way to so many requests that he was now calling a halt to any further expenditure – or, as he somewhat dramatically put it to senior management, "I am at the end of my spending indulgence!"

## 1955

The year was to prove a most momentous one for the Union-Castle Mail Steamship Company Limited. But before covering the drama that was to unfold in the latter half of 1955, I would like to recall the holiday of a lifetime the Damant family enjoyed that summer.

Although I frequently escorted parties of travel agents to Southampton to stay overnight on board the mailship prior to her sailing the next day, to show them over the vessel, and to wine and dine them in true Union-Castle style, this – excellent as it was - did not equate with an actual voyage. I felt that, to do my job properly, I should be able to speak of sailing Union-Castle from actual experience, and using this argument, I applied to the powers that be for a voyage to the Atlantic Islands in the off-season of July 1955.

To our delight the application was agreed. The schedule I'd put forward involved the two latest mailships ordered by Sir Vernon Thomson in 1946 and ran like this: depart Southampton by *Edinburgh Castle* bound for the Cape via Las Palmas, where stay for six nights; then by Aquila Airways flying boat to Funchal, Madeira, where briefly stay at the famous Reid's Hotel prior to embarking on *Pretoria Castle* (Out of Africa) bound for Southampton.

We were in good company aboard the flagship for a delegation from the South and East African Shipping Conference was with us en route for Cape Town, where they were to negotiate freight rates with the South African Shipping Board. Since Union-Castle

In October 1941, in the darkest days of the war, I was to meet Linda and in June 1942 to marry her. Three years later as the last V2 bomb fell uncomfortably close to our home in Essex, our daughter Avril was born and, in 1948, our son Stephen. Together with their respective spouses they have over the years presented Linda and me with five lovely grandchildren, three boys and two girls. In June 2002 we celebrated our Diamond Wedding Anniversary with them.

was the leading line serving those parts, the Company's assistant managing director, John Bevan, was chairman of the conference and headed the party. The rest of the delegation was made up of Sir Nicholas Cayzer, vice chairman of Union-Castle's principal rivals on the freight side, the Clan Line, Laurie Woof, a Clan Line director, and from Union-Castle, Percy Lambert, a freight department head, and Joe Beckitt of the management secretariat.

Linda and I revelled in shipboard life, whilst our children, Avril (10) and Stephen (7) were in the safe hands of the children's hostess, who kept them amused throughout the day. The sheer enjoyment and relaxation we had from sitting on deck and just watching the ocean going by was truly remarkable for Linda and me. (It was Coard Miles Squarey, a man as elegant as his name who, seconded from Thomas Cook to head up Ocean Travel Development, coined the slogan , "at sea you can rest, relax and recuperate." How right he was. Once out at sea the ship becomes very much your own world, especially when you look north, south, east, and west and see only ocean. The good, clean, air, the excellent food and fine wines, and the superb service all add up to a feeling of great well being which it would be difficult to equal.

Sir Nicholas Cayzer, a tall and distinguished looking man, then aged 46, dressed usually in a well cut tweed sports jacket and flannels, endlessly paced the decks, obviously deep in thought.

Our last hours aboard the good ship *Edinburgh Castle* prior to docking at Las Palmas were memorable indeed. It was a warm, balmy, star-lit night and we sat out on deck in the forecourt of the verandah cafe, drinking champagne with Lambert and

The children's' hostess at work.

Beckitt. At 2 am we retired to our cabins and, looking through the porthole, there on the horizon, shimmering in the blackness of the night, were the lights of Las Palmas.

When we awoke about seven the view was far less romantic. We were alongside the quay which was a mass of pipes refuelling the liner for the ten day voyage to Cape Town. As regards an hotel, the de luxe *Santa Catalina* was well out of our reach, but a modest outlay of three shillings and sixpence (about seventeen pence now) on a little book published by Percival Marshall and entitled, "A Fortnight in Madeira and the Canaries" proved an invaluable investment. Written by the prolific travel writer Gordon Cooper, he strongly recommended the *Hotel Lentiscal* in Tafira, close to Las Palmas.

It proved an ideal choice. On arrival there we were greeted warmly by the proprietor, Otto Kercher, and his daughter Lotti. Kerchner was a dignified, white-haired Austrian probably in his late fifties. Lotti, thirty-ish was red haired, attractive, and very attentive. From the moment we arrived until the moment we left nothing was too much trouble.

The hotel's imposing white-walled facade gave no indication of the charms that lay within. At back of the Lentiscal, facing north-east, was the dining room where the windows offered a picturesque vista of the countryside and, in particular, the Angostura valley where the grapes from which the local muscadel wine is made, were growing. Our large bedrooms, immaculately clean, were simply equipped with solid-looking Spanish furniture. Linda and I had a double, and Avril and Stephen the same, with a private bathroom and toilet between the two rooms.

Once settled in we decided to sit out in the little garden at the back of the hotel. This was reached by a series of steep stone steps, the land on which the hotel was built falling away sharply until it met, some five hundred yards away, another road running parallel with Tafira's main street. Then the ground rose again sharply across terraced fields to the hills beyond. The time was now nearing eleven, and Linda fancied coffee and the children lemonade. I made my way back up the steps to reception, asked for the drinks, and almost as soon as I had returned to the garden, was followed by some half a dozen waiters and waitresses who successfully negotiated the difficult steps not only with the drinks, but also carrying a circular table and four chairs.

*Linda in the garden at the Lentiscal Hotel, Las Palmas.*

On the stroke of eleven from across the fields came the deep throated blast of the *Edinburgh Castle's* sirens as she left the port of Las Palmas for South Africa. In the few hours we had been in Las Palmas everything had seemed so strange. Linda had loved every second on board the ship and had been loathe to leave. Now, hearing that siren, she was close to tears. It was, after all, our first venture abroad, and staying inland some eight miles from Las Palmas we felt very much foreigners – almost pioneers, being the only Brits around. As such we were a constant source of interest to the locals, particularly to the many children, but like all Spanish people, they had perfect manners, albeit an unquenchable curiosity.

Luncheon did little to relieve Linda's despondency. Although perfectly presented with the most attentive service, her typically Spanish starter convinced Linda she should have stowed away on *Edinburgh Castle*. It consisted of a single raw egg floating in a brown soup in a circular earthenware dish – and it looked straight back at her like some great baleful eye. But, by late afternoon, Linda was beginning to relish the prospect before us – of Spanish sunshine and the warm hospitality of the local people.

Before dinner that evening Cecil Pavillard of Union-Castle's local agents, Elder Dempster (Las Palmas) Ltd., called on us. He told us he had put a car and chauffeur at our disposal for the duration of our stay in Grand Canary, and that from time to time as his work permitted, he would accompany us on tours around the island.

At about ten the next morning the car duly reported to the *Lentiscal*. Our driver, who answered to the name Butch, looked like a somewhat beaten up boxer, but just the sort of guy to have on your side in the event of a punch up. Actually he was gentleness itself, grinned a lot, and adored the two children. Like all car drivers on the island, he always drove as if there was a lap record to be broken or, at least, a train to catch. I drew some comfort from the large St. Christopher medallion which swung to and fro on a chain from the ignition key as we tore along the narrow roads.

Because of the children, much of our time was spent on the beautiful las Canteras

*Shore of Las Canteras – Las Palmas de Gran Canaria.*

beach where the sun was so hot that it was uncomfortable to walk on the firm sand with bare feet. Prior to our first visit we were solemnly warned about observance of the local proprieties. "If you put so much as one foot on the promenade without your shirt on the police will throw you back on the beach," I was told.

"And there must be no changing on the beach; you should hire a *caseta*." This was a beach tent and they came in two sizes – grande and pequeño. The grande size was a splendid affair and fully justified the expenditure of a few extra pesetas. With it you got two poles for affixing the front flap to, thus providing an excellent awning under which to retreat when the sun became too hot. Lotti Kercher would provide a picnic basket with a lunch of chicken, crisp bread, and fruit. The bathing was safe and the large expanse of beach far from crowded.

I do not know whether it was curiosity or necessity, or indeed a combination of both, which prompted Stephen to announce that

he wished to go to the loo. Nevertheless the request was made and I took him to the promenade to seek out the necessary. A near-by cafe/restaurant seemed a good bet. Inside, everyone from the proprietor down displayed the greatest interest in trying to unravel our problem and, eventually, I succeeded in making myself understood. We were then ushered down a dark, narrow, corridor and shown a door. Opening it somewhat gingerly we were greeted with a stark, cell-like room. In the middle of the floor was a hole, flanked on

*Our grande caseta.*

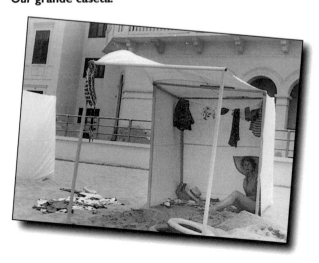

**20**

either side by a large footprint sunk into the concrete. Stephen quickly got the message and we emerged in triumph into the sunlight.

"The one excursion you should not miss is the one which takes you to Cruz de Tejeda" wrote Gordon Cooper in his invaluable little guide book. How right he was. Gran Canaria is the result of a volcanic eruption and is shaped roughly like a cone. The peak of the cone is Cruz de Tejeda, twenty-three miles from Las Palmas and 5000 feet above sea level. On the outward trip you climb almost the whole way up a steep mountain road with, often, a sheer drop on one side. Rough wooden crosses set at intervals along the roadside caught my attention and I asked Pavillard their significance. I was told they marked the spots where over-ambitious drivers had run out of road and plunged to their deaths in the ravine below. We climbed higher and higher and at one stage I noticed a funeral cortege far below. The ornate hearse was drawn by black horses with plumes on their heads, and a little procession of black clad mourners followed behind.

Halfway up to the Cruz de Tejeda Pavillard suggested we might like to try the local wine and we pulled up alongside some white-walled buildings, in one of which was a simple open doorway. Coming out of the glaring sunshine, our eyes took a little time to adjust to the dimness of the interior. Down one side ran a bar, against which were leaning two Spaniards. They wore broad-brimmed straw hats, were unshaven, and looked for all the world like bandits. They were eating lumps of meat which they took with their fingers from a bowl of oil. They looked a pretty fearsome sight and although the children did not exactly cling to their mother's skirts, we were somewhat relieved when they drew themselves up, raised their hats, and solemnly bid us "Buenos dias". The same simple courtesy was extended to us when we left.

Hair-raising as the journey occasionally was, I had by now considerable faith in Butch and St. Christopher. Certainly any

brief frights we had en route were more than compensated for by the many pleasures that awaited us at the end of the journey. "A chaos of grandeur" was how Cooper described the superb view with, towards the horizon, the sea sparkling in the sunlight and rising out of it, seemingly within walking distance, the island of Tenerife. A most memorable luncheon was had at the state-owned Parador

We had had many surprises during our stay in Grand Canary. The most pleasant was awaiting us at dinner on our final evening. We entered the *Lentiscal* dining room and caught our breath. Our table had lighted candles on it and between the places laid for the meal were lines of beautiful red and white flower heads leading into a central floral decoration. Behind stood smiling Mr. Kercher and his daughter. She explained, "We always do this for our guests on their last night with us."

Settling our bill the next morning proved yet another pleasant surprise. Two double rooms with inter-connecting private bathroom and toilet, plus most meals for six nights – under £30! On my return to the office I arranged for the *Hotel Lentiscal* to be added to the list of hotels recommended by Union-Castle in their brochure covering holidays in Las Palmas. Some years later I learned from the Spanish Tourist Office in London that there is now no Hotel Lentiscal in Tafira Alta. What, I wonder, became of that elegant Austrian gentleman and his charming red-haired daughter, but sadly, we never found out.

Not only was this our first trip abroad, but the link between Las Palmas and Madeira provided by Alquila Airways was also our first flight.

We had been provided by the airline with a comprehensive *Handbook of Information for Passengers* and I read it from cover to cover, which was just as well. From it I learned it was normal procedure for the pilot to make two dummy runs across the water

before becoming airborne after the third run. Had we not known this, the heavy revving of the engines, followed by a hectic race across the water, ending in the plane not rising by so much as an inch off the sea would have been most disconcerting to say the least. As it was, once we rose into the air following the third run, all our fellow passengers, who were either Spanish or Portuguese, crossed themselves.

By 2 pm Alquila Airways' flying boat *Irma Awatere* was a hundred miles north of Las Palmas travelling at a grand speed of 150

*Boarding the flying boat.*

**Reid's Hotel,** *Funchal, Madeira – in the 'fifties'.*

mph at a height above sea level of 6500 feet. We were fifteen minutes ahead of schedule and Captain Pearson estimated our time of arrival at Funchal, Madeira, as 5.15 pm.

As we began our run-in to Funchal I received an invitation to join the Captain on the flight deck. It was a thrilling sight circling over the bay and we passed low over the *Winchester Castle* which was getting up steam prior to leaving for the Cape, having sailed from Southampton three days earlier. She looked like a giant model.

Asked to list the top ten to twelve hotels in the world one would almost certainly include *Reid's Hotel*, Madeira. It is now known as *Reid's Palace Hotel*, once it had been acquired by Orient Express Hotels, who also own another top-ten hotel, the famous *Mount Nelson*, in Cape Town. *Reid's* is on a superb site on the cliff top at one corner of Funchal Bay, with the hotel itself surrounded on three sides by the most fabulous tropical gardens, and the accommodation, food and service are all of a standard of excellence it would be difficult to surpass.

July is 'out of season' as far as Madeira is concerned, their 'busy season' being our winter months. This has major benefits for us.

Firstly, we were allocated the most impressive suite of rooms, those in fact occupied by Churchill five years earlier when he had spent a painting holiday on the island. Secondly, since no staff had been laid off, service was overwhelmingly par excellence with about ten waiters hovering at mealtime. Thirdly, all the hotel's many, many, facilities were available to the extent that, for example, the swimming pool (reached by a lift down the cliff face) was ours and ours alone.

*Avril and Stephen on the balcony of the 'Churchill Suite', Reid's Hotel, Madeira.*

It has, incidentally, to be recorded that once in our magnificent suite of rooms, Linda started unpacking to discover to her horror, everything, but everything, soaked in gin! That splendid bottle of Gordon's Export gin placed in our cabin the day we left Southampton was still half full when we packed in Las Palmas and we were certainly not going to leave it behind. For reasons which I have now forgotten, Linda kindly volunteered to take it in her case. By the time it had been loaded and offloaded in taxis, launches, flying boat, etc., and at no time very gently – it was little wonder that the bottle, carefully cushioned as it had been, in bras, underwear and the like, had broken.

Apart from the intoxicating smell of gin and the various garments soaked in it, there were the bits of broken glass. Happily the label on the bottle had to some extent held the shattered pieces together; nevertheless, everything had to be gone through with the utmost care. Eventually, we went down to dinner with Linda wearing but one perfume – gin

We were additionally fortunate in that our own short stay on the island coincided with a visit there by Mr and Mrs Gordon Brown. Since 1934 Gordon Brown had edited the Year Book and Guide to Southern Africa, produced annually for Union-Castle. Each year Mr. and Mrs Brown spent six months at the Cape (in their summer months) and the rest of the year in the UK (in our summer months). I must confess that, to me, this seemed like paradise, particularly as it necessitated four voyages (eight weeks at sea) a year.

They were kindness itself to us and used their great knowledge of the island to enable us to see as much as possible during the limited time of our stay. In this comparatively short time it seemed to me that everyone had come up to us with hand outstretched. This was in complete contrast to our experience in Gran Canaria where no

*Mrs Gordon Brown, left, returning to Reid's with Linda after a shopping trip.*

one had begged at all. I mentioned this to Gordon Brown who expressed little or no surprise at my comment, saying that recently he had been in Funchal Cathedral where he had been approached by a man who tried to sell him dirty postcards. There was, nevertheless, great beauty on the island and our stay was all too short.

The scene in Funchal Bay prior to our sailing for home in the *Pretoria Castle* resembled some Eastern Bazaar. Not only were there innumerable vendors actually on board the ship with their wares spread out on deck but, in addition, the vessel was surrounded by a flotilla of rowing boats. Some offered a variety of goods including the exquisite local lace work, whilst the occupants of others would dive into the water for coins thrown from on board.

Linda and I were prepared for a very quiet voyage home. After all, we had argued, everyone will have made their friends during the ten day voyage from Cape Town. Nothing could have been further from the truth. We were new faces and just about everybody wanted to make our acquaintance. We were invited to all the cocktail parties and had a great time – the perfect end to that holiday of a lifetime.

THE YEAR BOOK AND GUIDE TO SOUTHERN AFRICA Edited annually by A. Gordon Brown, FRCS. I have a copy of the 1950 edition of the above and what a fascinating read it is.

For the princely sum of eight shillings and sixpence – less than 50p today – it is a book of 975 pages, of which some 750 cover general information and statistics, a large travel section, town plans, and a 48 page South African atlas.

Advertisements fill the rest of the pages and give an interesting insight to Southern Africa and, of course the Union-Castle line.

The various firms used by the company over many years are well represented – from Harland & Wolff of Belfast, who built the ships, to Heaton Tabb, who decorated and furnished them, and Monerrys, naval tailors for over one hundred years, who fitted out the ship's officers.

An extensive section is headed up by Cape Town's legendary *Mount Nelson Hotel*, where inclusive terms per person started at 27/6d a day – less than £1.40 today.

Some six months after the holiday, I was entering Head Office at 3, Fenchurch Street after calling on some agents in the city and stood to one side to allow what was obviously a deputation from the Clan Line to make their way out.

The party was led by their chairman, Lord Rotherwick, a dapper little man in his mid seventies, wearing a monocle, an impeccable suit, and –I noted with interest – dark blue suede shoes. Sir Nicholas was in the party, from which he detached himself to greet me and enquire how our holiday had gone after we had left the *Edinburgh Castle*. I resisted the temptation to ask what they were doing there, but only had to wait a few days for the answer. He was on the financial pages of all the nationals on 4 October 1955.

Clan Line and Union-Castle Line, they reported, had announced a scheme for the amalgamation of the share holdings of the two companies by means of an exchange of shares into a new holding company. Under the headline, 'Clan Line marry with Union-Castle rival - £53 m share swop', Frederick Ellis wrote: "Merger it may be announced as, but the financial arrangements make it a virtual take-over by Clan, for it will boss 60% of the new set up against Union-Castle's 40%. For Union-Castle, a sad day. It becomes junior partner on the African run it has dominated by speedy mail boats for over a century. The new holding company will have great management – for the Clan Line bosses are

The following account of an episode during the voyage out provides the perfect footnote to that oh-so-memorable holiday.

One afternoon I suggested a game of table tennis to Linda, who went back to the cabin to change from high heels to flat- heeled shoes. As I waited by the table for her return, Sir Nicholas Cayzer, on one of his many walks around deck, stopped and challenged me to a game.

We were in the midst of a hard fought 'best of three' when Linda returned, quickly sized up the situation, and discreetly withdrew. Having been beaten, Sir Nicholas then sought his revenge at deck golf, but once more emerged the loser. I found Linda and said, "Now there's a man I'd like to work for..." Some six months later I was doing just that.

supreme in the shipping business. Summing up – a take-over masquerading as a merger. Good for the Cayzers. Union-Castle appears to have no option but to accept the terms."

At the office that day the news was the sole topic of conversation. There were many rumours, some good, some bad. Joe Beckitt, the company's Cassandra, who had been with us on board Edinburgh Castle, maintained the worst was yet to come. The next four months were to see what was variously described as a 'dramatic battle for control' and 'a bitter and protracted struggle.'

The very next day, after the October 4 announcement, important Union-Castle shareholders headed by financier Harold Drayton and shipowner Jack Billmeir announced their opposition to the merger scheme and, on October 14 a committee was set up by the Company's ordinary shareholders to watch their interests.

A month later *The Times* reported that full details – seven pages long – of the proposed scheme for the merger of Clan and Union-Castle, together with a formal offer of the new holding company, The British and Commonwealth Shipping Company, to acquire the share capitals on an exchange basis had been forwarded to existing holders. Frederick Ellis (*Daily Express*) said he sympathised with the shareholders, "For they receive documents running into thousands of words – the marriage lines for the proposed wedding of the two companies."

On 30 November certain Union-Castle shareholders sought an injunction to restrain the directors from carrying on the scheme of amalgamation with Clan Line, alleging that the principle that the company should remain in British control was not sufficiently safeguarded, but after a five day hearing the motion was dismissed.

In early December an extraordinary General Meeting was called for January 1956, in a bid to remove the Union-Castle Board of Directors.

On the eve of Christmas 1955, in a temporary lull in the Castle versus Clan clash, the seemingly irrepressible, the certainly indefatigable Frederick Ellis headed his city column 'Santa Ellis hands out the presents'. "Each according to his lights", he handed out 'gifts' to those who had appeared in his columns during the year. After dishing out a brace of haloes to Motor Knights, Leonard Lord and Patrick Hennessy, for keeping their prices down, he wrote: "To Sir George Christopher, Union-Castle's chairman, a P.R.O. to see that what he sends to shareholders he also sends to city editors."

Exactly how much official notice, if indeed any, was taken of this I do not know. Nevertheless, in the new year I relinquished my agency duties on being appointed to the newly created post of Press Officer for the Union-Castle Line. There then followed some of the most interesting and rewarding years of my career.

I had strong feelings about Press Relations, just as I had had about the agents set-up, but more of that later. Meanwhile let us return to the chain of events leading up to the Cayzer' take over.◆

ALTHOUGH UNION-CASTLE was then at its zenith and boasted a fleet of twenty-eight ships, of which fifteen were luxury passenger liners, the signs of competition were already there. Opposite is the advertisement taken by South African Airways (the blue and silver fleet) in the *1950 Year Book and Guide to Southern Africa*.

# THE BRITISH & COMMONWEALTH

# SHIPPING COMPANY LIMITED

# REPORT & ACCOUNTS

# 1956

## CHAPTER TWO

# 'A TAKEOVER MASQUERADING AS A MERGER'*

*Comment in the national press*

## 1956

Two days before the January 5 extraordinary general meeting, the Cayzer family offered better terms with a £1 000 000 'gift' from their holdings. The meeting was duly held, and some two hundred Union-Castle shareholders learned formally that opposition to the proposed merger had been withdrawn following the increased offer to ordinary shareholders. "In a city office in dingy St. Mary Ave, heart of the shipping industry" wrote Ellis the next day, "one of the bitterest city merger struggles ended peacefully last night over cups of tea..."

On 2 February the Financial Times reported that the directors of British & Commonwealth Shipping Company had announced that by the close of business on 31 January acceptances of the November offer had been received from the holders of over 90% of the issued capital of the Union-Castle Line.

It was said that the Cayzers had waited nearly thirty years for this moment. Sir Vernon Thomson would have shown them the door had they dared to even mention such a thing as 'merging,' let alone, 'take over.'

Ironically, it was another Thomson who played the major part in gaining control of Union-Castle – James A. Thomson, CA., the Clan Line's financial director. He was almost certainly the principal author of the complex merger scheme. "But such things are Thomson's pride and joy," the *London Evening Standard* commented at the time.

The report went on: "Four years ago this modest, diffident Scot produced the toughest share plan the city had ever seen. He bought the Cayzer shipping family £5 000 000 of marketable shares, yet still left them in control of the Clan Shipping Line business."

That plan took Thomson eighteen months to think out and it needed fourteen closely printed pages to explain, but very few in the city really grasped its intricacies. In fact it was said that Thomson was the only man who understood them and that, it seems, included the Cayzer family too, for soon afterwards they put him on the Clan Line Board.

Despite the take-over – for take-over it was – Sir George Christopher boasted to his fellow directors that he would remain chairman in charge of Union-Castle until he was seventy, to which one of them retorted, "George, you'll be out in six months." Actually, it was four: on 3 May, to the surprise of almost nobody, Sir George tendered his resignation. In just over three years he had gained, and then lost, a veritable empire. Lord Rotherwick immediately took over as Union-Castle chairman, and his nephew, Sir Nicholas Cayzer, became deputy chairman.

Just over three weeks later, exciting plans for the future of the Union-Castle passenger service, were announced. It was revealed that negotiations were already in progress with ship builders Harland and Wolff

*Lord Rotherwick*

of Belfast "to alter, improve, and enlarge" the *Pendennis Castle*, the new mailship reluctantly ordered by Sir George Christopher in March 1955.

Describing itself as 'a comprehensive week-to-week review of political, industrial, and trade developments in all the territories of Southern Africa, and an advertising medium of sixty years standing,' the magazine

*South Africa* was published every Saturday. *South Africa's* revered editor, J.A.Gray, was the confidant for many years of Union-Castle's top brass. The *Daily Telegraph's* Jack Frost, doyen of the shipping reporters, was the only other journalist to be held in such high regard. Shortly after the merger Gray sought an interview with Lord Rotherwick. As the interview progressed Gray quickly began to realise that he was getting an exclusive.

Orders for new mailships had already been announced and were public knowledge, but Lord Rotherwick revealed they were planning to reduce the voyage time between Southampton and Cape Town to eleven and a half days and that only seven ships (as opposed to eight then in operation) would be required to run the accelerated service. The first most of us knew about this was when we read it in *South Africa*, not the sort of situation which pleases your Press Officer.

For Francis Keenlyside who, it will be remembered, had joined Union-Castle in 1947 on the clear understanding from Sir Vernon Thomson that he was the heir apparent, the take over by Clan Line was, to quote his own words, "The disaster of my life." The whole affair was, he said, "A misery to me." Not that he was not treated well by the new owners, but all the things he had set his heart on were over. Added to which he had been repeatedly approached during the struggle for power by the many leading figures in the city opposed to the merger to come out into the open on their side – with the promise of immediate appointment as managing director and succession as chairman. All this Keenlyside found most tempting but he refused to join their opposition. "My only reason," he told me, "was a Victorian scruple: I was an employee and as such it would be wrong of me to question the actions of my directors."

In mid-August further details were released, not only of the improvements being made in *Pendennis Castle*, but also of the first of the new mailships – a new Superliner. She was to be the biggest and best liner ever to enter the South African Trade – a new 38000 tonnes *Windsor Castle* (reviving an old Union-Castle name) – to be built by Cammell Laird of Birkenhead. This represented a considerable break with tradition as the Union-Castle mailships had since 1900 been built by Harland & Wolff. "Nothing like a change on the bridge for new ideas," commented one journalist.

## 1957

An even greater break with tradition was the decision to quit 3 Fenchurch Street, London, EC 3, for so long Union-Castle's head office.

The opponents of the merger – and there were quite a few – saw in the decision a sort of 'we are the masters now' gesture on the part of the Clan Line. Yet, in fairness, Union-Castle was the last major shipping company to have its principal passenger booking office in the city and not in the West End of London, and this was undoubtedly one of the main reasons for the move.

The passenger and publicity departments moved to palatial new offices named Rotherwick House at 19-21 Old Bond Street, London, W.1. After working for over twenty years in the city I was, for the first time, working in the West End.

The *London Evening Standard's* shipping correspondent Gordon Holman wrote: "By 7 October 1957 the building on the corner of Fenchurch Street, which has housed Union-Castle Line (and its predecessors) for eighty-four years will close down, and the red, white, and blue flag known the world over, will be lowered from the tall city building."

Two days later, the *Daily Telegraph's* Peterborough under the heading, "On Board in Bond Street," recounted in his diary: "Lord and Lady Rotherwick were 'at home' last night at 19 Bond Street. These new Mayfair offices of the Union-Castle Line, of which Lord Rotherwick is chairman, are designed and decorated in the latest luxury liner style." A bit gushing, perhaps, for Peterborough, but the fact remained that the new premises were indeed magnificent.

The decision to open a West End office had presented the perfect opportunity of re-establishing the Union-Castle Passenger Department on modern and efficient lines, not only as regards layout and decor, but also from the point of view of service to clients, internal administration and booking procedures, the last a favourite hobby-horse of mine back in the agency days. Certainly, as the last major shipping company to open an office in the West End, we had one advantage – that of learning from the experience of others.

As the advertisement Union-Castle took in *The Times* on opening day of the new chief passenger office truly stated: "No effort has been spared in laying out a booking hall second to none in which customers can be served with courtesy and in comfort."

I was only to be a short while at the new offices as, to my high delight, I was asked to set up an entirely new department for the group covering, not only press but also public relations, and to operate from Head Office in the city, where I was to be directly responsible to the Chairman and Deputy Chairman. My brief, quite simply, was to put over the message to as many people as possible that it was now FUN to sail Union-Castle.

## 1958

Early in the year Lord and Lady Rotherwick decided to make Union-Castle's famous "Round Africa" voyage. I was instructed to be present at the party in their suite prior to sailing and to bring a photographer with me to take pictures to send to the glossy society magazines The photographs, which subsequently appeared in, for example, the *Tatler & Bystander*, portrayed a happy occasion with champagne and laughter as the family wished Uncle Bertie Bon Voyage.

However, it was to be one of the last such occasions, for Lord Rotherwick became ill during the voyage. He was put ashore at Aden and flown home, where, on 18 March, three months after going to Belfast with his wife to name the largest ship he had ever built, he died.

Peterborough of the *Daily Telegraph* telephoned to ask what sort of a man Lord Rotherwick was. I described how I had first seen him at 3 Fenchurch Street over two years ago – monocle, impeccable suit, and dark blue suede shoe The next day, under the heading 'Elegant Shipowner', I was amused to find Peterborough writing as follows:

Lord Rotherwick, whose death has been announced at the age of seventy-six, never adopted the rich man's affectation of dressing like a poor one. Of extremely short stature with his eyeglass and perfectly cut clothes, he was always the picture of elegance. When I saw him as he was leaving in January on what was to be his last cruise, he wore a suit with narrow trousers and youthfully sporty suede shoes.

Sir Nicholas Cayzer succeeded his uncle as chairman of the group, and his brother, Mr. Bernard Cayzer, the new Lord Rotherwick (the former Hon. Robin Cayzer), and his brother, the Hon. Anthony Cayzer, all become deputy chairmen. All this time Francis Keenlyside had continued to soldier on, attending regular management meetings, at which he said, "I made a number of points with my customary directness."

One such meeting was called by the chairman, Sir Nicholas Cayzer, to discuss arrangements for deputy chairman Bernard Cayzer's forthcoming visit to America to call on travel agents there. Present were the other deputy chairman Anthony Cayzer, a passenger manager Geoff Speight, a publicity manager Arthur Robson and myself. It was agreed the visit would start with a top-class reception in New York and discussion continued on various aspects of the proposed event. "Perhaps," said Anthony Cayzer, "we could have soft music playing in the background," at which Keenlyside threw back his head and roared with laughter! Sadly, he was asked to no more meetings, the Cayzers being very wary of him from then on.

Inevitably, Keenlyside left the company and took up a new career in the United States, from where he eventually retired to Andorra to write *Peaks and Pioneers*, the definitive work on the history of mountaineering, which was his great love. It was a pleasure to have known Francis Keenlyside, a man from whom I learned much.

The top management set-up of Sir Nicholas (later to become Lord) Cayzer as chairman with his three deputies was to continue until the cessation of the mail service in 1977.◆

## CHAPTER THREE

## LAUNCHES

### Pretoria Castle and

### Edinburgh Castle – 1947

The two big ships announced by Sir Vernon Thomson when he clinched the mail contract in 1945 were now ready for launching and it was indicative of his great love for ships that he made these two events so memorable.

Each ship had a gross tonnage of 28 705 and were then the largest vessels ever in the Union-Castle fleet. They each carried 227 First and 478 Cabin class passengers.

*Pretoria Castle* was named and launched on 19 August 1947 by Mrs Smuts, wife of Field-Marshall Smuts, the South African Prime Minister, pressing a button in her home near Pretoria some 6 000 miles from the Belfast shipyards of Harland & Wolff. Electric impulses over a land line to Cape Town, directed by radio to London and re-transmitted to Belfast not only caused the bottle of Cape Sparkling wine to break on the bow of the ship, but also started her on her way.

The late King George VI and Queen Elizabeth with their two daughters, the present Queen and the late Princess Margaret, had visited South Africa in the spring of

Sir Vernon Thomson, whose speeches at the luncheons following the launch of the half a dozen passenger ships he had been responsible for ordering, followed more or less the same lines, but always included the following:

"Did you notice," he would say, "when the ship left the ways and took the water how she curtsied in stately fashion to the gracious lady who had just named her?"

31

UNION-CASTLE LINE TO SOUTH AND EAST AFRICA.

THE UNION-CASTLE ROYAL MAIL STEAMER "PRETORIA CASTLE" 28.705 TONS

*RHODESIA CASTLE*
(17 041 grt)
500 Passengers -
launched 5 April 1951

*KENYA CASTLE*
(17 041 grt)
530 Passengers -
launched 21 June 1951

*BRAEMAR CASTLE*
(17 029 grt)
556 passengers -
launched 24 April 1952

1947, so it was appropriate that *Pretoria Castle's* sister ship, *Edinburgh Castle* be named and launched in Belfast on 16 October 1947 by Princess Margaret – her first major public engagement.

It was noteworthy that each of these new vessels cost approximately £3 million to build. By 1953 each would have cost over £6 million.

## Bloemfontein Castle – 1949

The 18 400 grt *Bloemfontein Castle* was launched at Belfast by Mrs Leif Egeland wife of the High Commissioner in London for South Africa, on 25 August 1949. Built for an expected emigrant boom to South and East Africa, she was the first single-class vessel to be ordered by Union-Castle and had accommodation for 739 passengers.

At the launching it was announced that these new one-class ships, based on the design of the *Bloemfontein Castle* but slightly smaller, were to be ordered, so completing the Line's post-war building schedule they were destined for the 'Round Africa' service:

It is interesting to recall that at the launch of *Bloemfontein Castle*, Sir Vernon Thomson called on the shipbuilding industry to get prices down by building ships faster, "Even if it means scrapping the five day week." This plea for Saturday working was received in polite silence by the many shipyard workers present. One wonders how such a plea would be received today.

## Pendennis Castle – 1957

Towards the end of the year the 'new improved' *Pendennis Castle* was ready for launching. Although she was to be engaged on what is recognised as a 'fair weather route' the Cayzers decided to fit Denny-Brown stabilisers to check rolling, so that even the dreaded Bay of Biscay would be robbed of its terrors. Fitting the stabilisers necessitated lengthening the vessel amidships after construction had commenced on the slipway. This most unusual operation represented a remarkable feat of engineering skill.

In addition the increased speed to be given to *Pendennis Castle* to enable her to cut the voyage time from fourteen to eleven days as was intended called for lengthening and fining the forward part of the hull. The overall length was in fact increased from 748 feet to 764 feet. Other vital statistics of the new liner were:

Gross tonnage : 28 453 tonnes
Passengers carried : First class 182
       Tourist class 493
Cargo carried : 581 979 cubic feet

But the big, exciting change was to be in the decor, which was to cut right across the traditional furnishings and decoration of all previous Union-Castle mailships. This new concept was the responsibility of Bernard Cayzer, younger brother of Sir Nicholas and a deputy chairman of the Line. He was assisted in this by a decorative assistant, the well known interior decorator Jean Monro. Their aim, they said, was to convey 'tranquillity and airy spaciousness.'

Towards the end of 1957 the 'new improved' *Pendennis Castle* was ready to be launched, and on a bitterly cold day in early December Lady Rotherwick, the chairman's wife, travelled to Belfast with a party of family and friends. There was only a small press party, which was probably just as well since there was to be no launch.

At Harland & Wolff's shipyard Lady Rotherwick, amid a flurry of snow, named "this ship *Pendennis Castle*", which, instead of then gliding gracefully into the water remained stubbornly where she was. The ship did not move because of a lightning strike. The sixteen who were due to knock the chocks out from under the ship refused to do so. At the luncheon afterwards Lord Rotherwick said he would never have a ship built in Belfast again. He was true to his word, so breaking with the decision of Sir Donald Currie, Union-Castle's first chairman, taken over fifty years previously, to have all mailships built in Belfast. The party returned to London and fifteen days later – on Christmas Eve 1957 – the *Pendennis*

*Castle* was quietly launched without ceremony. This unspectacular beginning in no way overshadowed the excited interest this beautiful ship was subsequently to arouse.

### *Windsor Castle – 1959*

Two weeks into 1959, with *Pendennis Castle* being fêted at the Cape on arrival there on her maiden voyage, the announcement was made to the world that *Windsor Castle* was to be named and launched on 23 June 1959 at Cammell Laird's Birkenhead shipyard by no less a personage than her Majesty Queen Elizabeth the Queen Mother. Not only was this the largest passenger liner ever built on Merseyside, but she was the largest to be launched at a British shipyard since the Cunard Line's *Queen Elizabeth* in 1938. She was to cost over ten million pounds and was scheduled to make her maiden voyage in August 1960.

There was to be 'spacious accommodation' for 250 First class and 600 Tourist class passengers. All passenger *and* crew cabins were to be air conditioned, as were the dining saloons, hairdressing salons, and cinema. The cinema, seating 250, was to be fitted with cinemascope equipment.

The Tourist class public rooms (other than the dining saloon) and recreation spaces occupied an entire deck, with a lounge facing

**Pendennis Castle**

OVER TEN YEARS LATER I was privileged, as one of only eighty members of the London Press Club, of which I was by then a member to meet the Queen Mother again, having been proposed by the *Daily Telegraph's* shipping correspondent Jack Frost.

THE UNION-CASTLE MAIL
STEAMSHIP COMPANY, LTD.
_____

Programme of Arrangements
for guests attending the launch of
R.M.S.
" WINDSOR CASTLE "
(38,000 tons approx.)
by
HER MAJESTY QUEEN ELIZABETH
THE QUEEN MOTHER
at the Shipyard of Cammell Laird and Co.
(Shipbuilders & Engineers) Ltd.,
Birkenhead.
on
TUESDAY, 23rd JUNE, 1959
at 1.30 p.m.

H. C. C. Damant, Esq.

*Please keep this programme for reference.*

CAMMELL LAIRD AND COMPANY (Shipbuilders & Engineers) LIMITED.
LAUNCH OF
R.M.S. "WINDSOR CASTLE"
By Her Majesty
QUEEN ELIZABETH THE QUEEN MOTHER
ON TUESDAY, 23rd JUNE, 1959.
ADMIT ONE
VIA MAIN ENTRANCE TO SHIPYARD (GREEN LANE GATE)
TO
PLATFORM AND PRESS LUNCHEON ROOM.
VISITORS SHOULD BE IN THEIR PLACES NOT LATER THAN 12-45 P.M.

The occasion was to mark the decision to allow ladies to join the club and to install Her Majesty as the first such member.

If I admired her that hot June afternoon in Birkenhead, I certainly admired her on that evening when, patient and charming, she worked her way round each and every one of the eighty of us, with all of whom she spent at least two minutes.

I was by then with the South African Wine Farmers Association in London, and when my turn came, she spoke warmly of Cape wines. I then said, "The only previous occasion I have had the pleasure of meeting you, Ma'am, was when you launched the *Windsor Castle* and caused us all consternation by having a nose-bleed at the last moment."

"Oh yes," said the Queen Mother, "I remember. Do you know, that's the only time I've ever had a nose bleed."

forward. In other words, even those paying the lowest rate of fare would be able to face forward in the lounge and no longer have their backs to the engine. There were also to be an open air swimming pool and verandah-cum lido area for each class, a medical centre with a highly qualified medical director, and stabilisers to minimise rolling. An innovation was

to be the provision of a special garage for passengers' cars. The crew would number 470 of whom 30 would be women. In addition to the Captain, *Windsor* was to carry a staff captain.

Union-Castle chairman, Sir Nicholas Cayzer, summed it up like this: "In this new ship we have tried to cater for the comfort and amusement of our passengers, to provide a ship that is colourful and pleasing to the eye and gives a sense of rest and repose." All this aroused tremendous interest, but particularly exciting was BBC Television's decision to cover the launch live, the first time the naming and launching of a great liner had received such coverage. Wynford Vaughan-Thomas was named as commentator for the event.

Tuesday 23 June 1959 dawned as one of those that obviously prompted a certain poet to commence his composition with the words, "Oh to be in England now...", although I fully appreciate he was referring to two months earlier. The sun shone, the sky was blue, and we all tackled full English breakfasts with enthusiasm on the 7.45 am special train from Euston to Liverpool by which the launch party and the media were travelling. We arrived at 11.30 am at Lime Street station. Coaches took us over to the shipyard at Birkenhead where the press party and I were on the launch platform by 12.45 am ready for the ceremony.

The Queen Mother was scheduled to name and launch the vessel at 1.30 pm. At 1.25 pm she suffered a sudden nosebleed, and consternation reigned. The majority of those present were completely oblivious of what was happening behind the scenes where, let it be said, the calmest person was the Queen Mother. Happily, she was able to emerge only a minute or so late, looking as though noth-

ing had happened, though the more observant might have detected the odd spot of blood on her dress. A great roar of applause greeted her as she came on to the platform, from where she successfully carried out the launching ceremony in magnificent style.

By 1.45 pm we had left the launching platform and were enjoying the buffet luncheon. Her Majesty left the shipyard at 3.30 pm and, ten minutes later we left by coach for afternoon tea at Liverpool's Adelphi Hotel.

The party had been booked to return to London by the 5.15 pm train from Lime Street station. Dinner was served during the journey and I had the good fortune to be seated with Wynford Vaughan-Thomas. I understand that in his native South Wales he is known as "Thomas the Talk". Certainly he had a fund of stories and anecdotes and throughout the journey back to town he regaled me with the most fabulous of tales covering his schooldays and his time spent in the Home Guard. All joyous, delightful stuff which I lapped up.

I suppose the story I enjoyed most concerned the schooldays of the famous Welsh poet, Dylan Thomas. He and a friend developed the habit of playing truant on certain afternoons to go into the village and play snooker. To do so they had to pass the headmaster's study and one day he burst out of the room crying, "Where are you boys

**RMS Windsor Castle**

going?" With bravado Dylan Thomas answered, "To the village to play snooker." The headmaster paused, and then said, "You wicked boys, I hope you get caught."

During the journey one of those bizarre incidents occurred that could have proved completely disastrous. Some idiot fired an air rifle at the train as it sped through the countryside and the pellet drilled a neat hole in the coach window about twelve inches above the head of Miss Nicola Cayzer, the chairman's daughter.

There was a story going the rounds that on a very wet and windy day in Greenock a Clan Line cargo ship was about to be launched. A member of the launch party called down to one of the many shipyard workers standing below, "I say, my man, have you a large mackintosh down there to cover two ladies?" to which he received the reply, "No Sir but we've a wee McGregor who's willing to try!"

It is a sad reflection of our so-called civilisation that a journalist from a leading national daily newspaper whispered to me, "This will guarantee the launch story on every front page!" It was apparently not enough that a British Shipping Company was prepared to invest some ten million pounds in a super new liner to make the front page – it needed the chairman's daughter to be nearly murdered to ensure that. The gorgeous Nicola Cayzer remained absolutely unruffled – and, yes, we got our front page coverage!

## Transvaal Castle – 1961

Built by John Brown & Company at Clydebank the 30 212 grt *Transvaal Castle* was launched on 17 January 1961 by Lady Cayzer, wife of Sir Nicholas, chairman of the British and Commonwealth Shipping Company and, of course, the Union-Castle Line.

She was the first one-class vessel to operate in the weekly mail service to the Cape and was known as an 'hotel class ship'. The standard of accommodation was regulated by price, but the public zones and all amenities were available to all passengers, for which there was accommodation for 728. *Transvaal Castle* was the first British liner to employ waitresses, or stewardettes as they were called.

## SA Vaal and SA Oranje – 1966

In late 1965 *Transvaal Castle* and *Pretoria Castle* (the youngest and oldest mailships) were transferred to Safmarine (South African Marine Corporation Ltd) and their sale was effected on 1 January 1966.

*Transvaal Castle* was renamed *SA Vaal* at Cape Town on 12 January 1966 by Mrs. CR Swart, the wife of the State President.

*Pretoria Castle* was renamed *SA Oranje* at Cape Town on 2 February 1966 by Mrs. HF Verwoerd, the wife of the South African Prime Minister.◆

**Transvaal Castle** *in Safmarine livery having been re-named* **SA Vaal** *to become South Africa's first mailship.*

# CHAPTER FOUR

## SHAKE-DOWN CRUISES

Once a ship has been launched, the builders take her out to sea to undergo tests on every piece of equipment. When they are satisfied the new ship meets their every requirement, she is handed over to the owners for a *shake down cruise*, when every facility on board is again put to the test, but on this occasion with a full complement of passengers. The passenger list is usually made up of VIPs, government officials, top representatives of the shipping lines, travel agents, and the media.

### 1893

Sir Donald Currie, who would be described today as an entrepreneur, was a giant in the shipping world of the day. In 1872 he founded the Castle Line and, four years later, was sharing the mail contract to South Africa with his great rival, the Union Line, until, after intense rivalry, they merged in 1900 to form the Union-Castle Line.

Currie had a natural flair for publicity as was shown by the shake down cruise he organised in 1893 for the 3946 tonnes *Pembroke Castle*, the first four masted steamer of the Castle Line. The passenger list included the Prime Minister, Gladstone, and the then aged poet laureate, Lord Tennyson. It seems that all were having such a good time that the cruise went on longer than intended and *Pembroke Castle* lay at anchor for several days at Copenhagen, where the celebrations continued with the ship's company being invited to the Royal Palace. Naturally, Currie reciprocated and laid on a veritable banquet on board, which was attended by, amongst others, the Czar, twenty-four Royal personages, and sixteen high ranking service

*Sir Donald Currie*

officers. After the great dinner Tennyson recited poems. Once *Pembroke Castle* returned to England Gladstone found he was in trouble – he had failed to inform the Queen he would be out of the country. Queen Victoria was not amused

### 1950

In the case of the *Bloemfontein Castle's* shake down cruise at the end of March 1950, the chairman's guests were 250 staff members from the London and Southampton offices of Union-Castle – an inspired piece of good staff relations on Sir Vernon's part.

For many this was their first sea voyage ever, and the *London Evening Standard's* Gordon Holman headed his piece: 'Cargo is – typists.' On the first morning at sea one young typist looked long and hard at the extensive breakfast menu and then said solemnly to the steward waiting to take her order, "I think I'll have a little of everything." Another was heard to exclaim, "Isn't it exciting? I can feel the spray coming in through the porthole." It was, in fact, an eager young clerk on the next table tackling his grapefruit with gusto.

### 1958

On 14 November 1958, following her successful sea trials, the *Pendennis Castle* was taken over by the Union-Castle Line and everything was set for her shake down cruise. The proposed guest list was made up of the usual personnel and I had come up with the somewhat revolutionary idea that wives be included on this occasion. The suggestion was approved.

That the recommendation was right was best borne out by the *Manchester Guardian's* shipping correspondent, Hardy Cutley, who, in his letter of thanks after the trip, wrote: "… the idea of inviting wives was a truly brilliant one. So often do we return home and regale our ladies with the joys they could have shared. In this matter, I am told, you have badly spiked the guns, or should it be 'stolen the wind', from another notable line."

*Pendennis Castle* was anchored in the Clyde off Gourock, where the cruise party arrived by special train on Saturday 29 November to find the whole Glasgow area shrouded in thick fog. Not even a Highlander in full regalia to pipe us aboard the tender at the pierhead did much to raise our spirits. As we set off, everything seemed so silent, dark, and indeed, miserable. Suddenly, out of the darkness, loomed a vast shape – *Pendennis Castle*, all 28 453 tonnes of her. Once on board everything was light, bright, and cheerful. The bars – all of them – were open and as we sat down to dine we were surprised to find we were under way and had been for some time.

The next day, Sunday, it had been arranged that deputy chairman Bernard Cayzer, who had masterminded so much of

*Mr Bernard Cayzer*

what had gone into the making of this undoubtedly beautiful ship, should hold a press conference in his suite on board. Special facilities, such as extra telephones, had been at the disposal of the journalists so there need be no delay in filing their stories with their respective journals. At 11.30am on 30 November 1958 most of the pressmen aboard – who numbered fifty three in all – arrived at the suite to be greeted by Bernard Cayzer, who then passed them on to his steward to ascertain their refreshment requirements. The conference itself was a triumph with Cayzer completely relaxed and

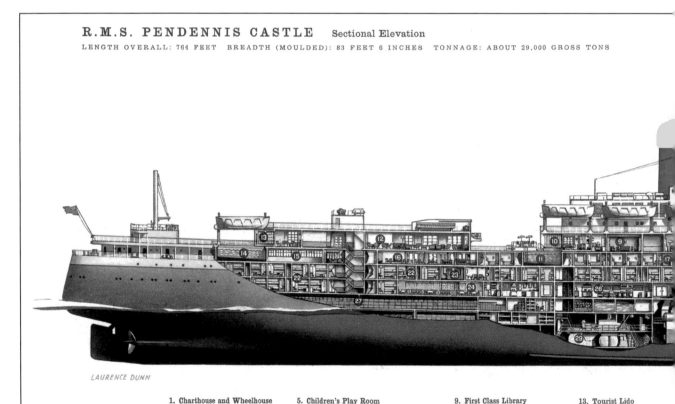

**R.M.S. PENDENNIS CASTLE** Sectional Elevation

LENGTH OVERALL: 764 FEET   BREADTH (MOULDED): 83 FEET 6 INCHES   TONNAGE: ABOUT 29,000 GROSS TONS

LAURENCE DUNN

| | | | |
|---|---|---|---|
| 1. Charthouse and Wheelhouse | 5. Children's Play Room | 9. First Class Library | 13. Tourist Lido |
| 2. Captain's Day Room | 6. First Class Lounge | 10. First Class Lido | 14. Tourist Swimming Pool |
| 3. Radio Room | 7. First Class Smoke Room | 11. First Class Swimming Pool | 15. Tourist Recreation Spac[e] |
| 4. Officers' Accommodation | 8. First Class Card and Writing Room | 12. Tourist Lounge | 16. Tourist Smoke Room |

ready to answer any question. As one journalist subsequently recorded: "I thought the press conference was unusually effective probably on account of the frankness of the replies given, notably on the question of costs, about which ship owners are inclined to be reticent."

*Pendennis Castle* docked at Southampton early on the Monday morning and the day's newspapers were brought on board at breakfast time to be avidly scanned and read. What was particularly pleasing was that each shipping correspondent had taken a different aspect of the new ship from which to major in his article, added to which the words 'fun' and 'funship' were beginning, increasingly, to be used. "If the fun," one correspondent wrote, "that Mr Bernard Cayzer talked about giving the passengers, bares any relation to the kind of fun we personally had on board, my wife and I can but envy the regular voyagers on the route."

Anthony Sampson, author of the much praised book *The New Anatomy of Britain*, was at that time writing a weekly diary piece for *The Observer* under the title of *Table Talk* and – would you believe – under the pen name 'Pendennis'. Naturally he was with us on the cruise and headed his subsequent piece *Pendennis Afloat* with a photograph of the new liner on her trials.

After a lengthy comment on the decor and facilities, *Pendennis* went on: "But the new *Castle* is certainly more business like than her predecessors. The puritan killjoy tradition that used to dog the Union-Castle has been thrown overboard by the new management; the influence of air travel can be felt everywhere in the emphasis on fun, rather than getting there." He finished his article with a reference to the Cayzers who, he wrote, "Bought Union-Castle three years ago in a spectacular offer to the shareholders. Since then," he continued, "the four cousins,

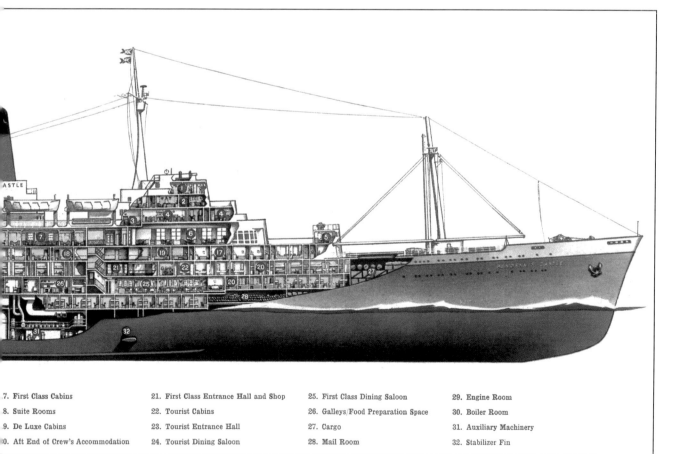

7. First Class Cabins
8. Suite Rooms
9. De Luxe Cabins
0. Aft End of Crew's Accommodation

21. First Class Entrance Hall and Shop
22. Tourist Cabins
23. Tourist Entrance Hall
24. Tourist Dining Saloon

25. First Class Dining Saloon
26. Galleys/Food Preparation Space
27. Cargo
28. Mail Room

29. Engine Room
30. Boiler Room
31. Auxiliary Machinery
32. Stabilizer Fin

who are all in their forties, have jazzed up the outfit a good deal, with a new glossy office in Bond Street and some spectacular salesmanship (the cousins were, in fact, brothers).

With *Pendennis Castle* now safely moored in Southampton it was possible to hold a series of luncheons on board at which to entertain and to show off the new liner to the many friends and contacts it had not been possible to invite on the shake down cruise. Such a luncheon was held on 5 December 1958 for the large Southampton press, radio, and television corps, and these events continued right up to New Year's Eve, the day before *Pendennis Castle* was to leave on her maiden voyage.

## 1960

Encouraged by the undoubted success of the shake down cruise for *Pendennis Castle* – and with, perhaps, thoughts of Sir Donald Currie's first voyage with *Pembroke Castle* in mind – plans were laid for a major five day

R.M.S. WINDSOR CASTLE

1. First Class Sun Deck.
2. First Class Children's Play Room.
3. Tourist Sun Deck.
4. First Class Lounge.
5. First Class Smoke Room.
6. Gymnasium.
7. First Class Bar.
8. First Class Verandah Café.
9. First Class Swimming Pool.
10. Garage.
11. Tourist Lounge.
12. Pantry and Kiosk.
13. Tourist Library.
14. Tourist Smoke Room.
15. Tourist Class Bar.
16. Tourist Recreation Space.
17. Tourist Verandah Café.
18. Tourist Swimming Pool.
19. Tourist Children's Play Room.
20. First Class Dining Saloon.
21. First Class Cabins.
22. Cinema.
23. Tourist Dining Saloon.
24. Tourist Cabins.

**Deputy Chairman
Anthony Cayzer**

inaugural cruise from the shipyard in Birkenhead for *Windsor Castle*.

However, due to a seaman's dispute the trip had to be cancelled at the last minute and the ves- sel arrived at Southampton two days earlier than planned. Deputy chairman, Anthony Cayzer, who was in charge of the overall arrangements for what would have been a memorable voyage aboard the mailship, was furious. He was so incensed that he mixed his metaphors when he declared, "The unions have become a sacred cow and the sooner they are knocked off their perch the better."◆

*South African Airways' magazine featured the **Windsor Castle** on its front cover – a pleasant compliment from a major competitor.*

## CHAPTER FIVE

# MAIDEN VOYAGES

### Dane – 1857

When, in 1857, the Union Steamship Co. Ltd., secured the mail contract to South Africa, the company boasted a fleet of six small ships. The largest of these, the 530 tonne *Dane*, inaugurated the service in September of that year. Some forty-four days after leaving Southampton the ship's commander, Captain Strutt, must have breathed a sigh of relief as that most impressive of landmarks, Table Mountain, appeared on the horizon.

*Captain Strutt, Commander of the Dane, 1857.*

So keen was the Union Line to start operations that they allowed themselves little or no time in which to advertise the new service, with the result that the *Dane* carried cargo that brought in only £102 – and just six passengers occupied the cabins. Nevertheless, the annual subsidy was a useful £30,000, and on the initial homeward voyage income was nearly £1500 compared with the meagre £300 made on the outward leg.

The new service was destined to go from strength to strength and one hundred years later, would still be talked about as one of the greatest in maritime history.

### Dunotar Castle – 1890 and Scot – 1891

The Union Line had been in existence for nineteen years when there emerged on the Cape Shipping Scene the remarkable Donald Currie, who had founded the Castle Line to operate a similar service to that started by the *Dane*. The challenge was then on to pro-

*The record-breaking Scot in Cape Town Harbour 1891.*

**Dunottar Castle**

vide an even faster service and to build even larger mailships. The competition was intense, as witness the rivalry in 1890/91.

That year Currie put into service the *Dunotar Castle* of 5600 tonne and as such by far the largest ship on the Cape route. She had accommodation for 360 passengers and on her maiden voyage in October 1890 shattered the existing record time by completing the voyage in seventeen days, twenty hours.

Not to be outdone, that same year, the Union Line launched their answer to *Dunotar Castle*. Generally reckoned to be one of the most beautiful of Victorian steamships, the 6884 tonne *Scot* had accommodation for 408 passengers, and on her maiden voyage in July 1891 she lowered the record of her rival by more than a day. Then, in March, 1893, she made the Cape run in fourteen days, eighteen hours, fifty-seven minutes – a record that stood for some forty years.

**Athlone Castle** *sistership* **to Stirling Castle.**

## Athlone Castle
## and Stirling Castle – 1936

The amalgamation in 1900 of Union and Castle Lines heralded a period of consolidation and the development of a unique service, but voyage time was always of the essence.

The ten year mail contract agreed in 1936 called for the Southampton/Cape Town voyage and vice versa to be reduced to fourteen days. With admirable foresight Union-Castle had ordered two new liners designed to make the Cape sailing in under two weeks; they were to be named *Athlone Castle* and *Stirling Castle*. Their entry into service enabled Thursdays at 4 pm to be made the weekly sailing day and departure time.

On her maiden voyage the 25 554 tonne *Stirling Castle* made the passage to South Africa in thirteen days, six hours, thirty minutes, so breaking Scot's record of 1893.

## Pendennis Castle – 1959

Somewhat different to the first voyage to the Cape of the 530 tonne *Dane* was the maiden voyage over one hundred years later of the 28 453 tonne *Pendennis Castle* at 4 pm on Thursday 1 January 1959. The seal was set on the day by the announcement in the BBC news bulletin that morning of the award in the New Year's Honours list of the CBE to Captain George Mayhew, commodore of the Union-Castle fleet, who was commanding the new flagship on her first sailing to Cape Town.

This was coupled with the news that the shipping press had unanimously voted *Pendennis Castle* Ship of the Year. Certainly the coverage she had received following the shake down cruise had been most favourable. Stanley Bonnettt's full page article headed 'For the New Year....a New Ship' in the *Daily Mail* made excellent reading on the boat train down to Southampton, where all was excitement.

A last minute request on Christmas Eve to obtain some publicity for what was the first ever milk bar on board an ocean going liner resulted in my making an urgent phone call to the Milk Marketing Board, who were only too pleased to arrange for the Dairy Princess for Southern England to be on board prior to sailing to join the Commodore in the first milkshake to be prepared in the new bar.

Dairy Princess Marion Crocker duly arrived on board, with a couple of Milk Marketing Board publicity men to pose for photographs with the ever patient Commodore Mayhew. The pictures taken received wide coverage. One of them was headlined, "The Commodore celebrates his CBE in milk." The caption read, "Celebrating his award of the CBE is Commodore George Mayhew and sharing a milkshake with him on board *Pendennis Castle* is Dairy Princess Marion Crocker. A feature of the Tourist Class Lido area of the *Pendennis Castle*, which was about to sail on her maiden voyage to South Africa, is a milk bar. The Dairy Princess had been invited to the new liner by the Commodore to sample the first milk shake prepared on board." And, for good measure, the event was shown on television that night.

Eventually, after a long luncheon with the large media corps present that day, we began to go ashore as four o'clock approached. Both BBC and Southern television cameras were already set up on the quayside ready to film the new mailship's departure. Never had the Thursday afternoon ritual seemed so charged with excitement. As the hour approached a sudden silence fell and we found ourselves virtually talking in whispers.

The silence was broken, first by the peal of bells from the city's civic centre, and then on the first stroke of four, to be answered immediately by blasts from the sirens of *Pendennis Castle*. As though by magic she began to move away from the quay with a great roar of cheering from both those on board and ashore. We stood grouped there on the dockside watching the proud ship becoming ever smaller as she headed south. I noticed that some fifty yards away from us, standing all on his own, was chairman Sir Nicholas Cayzer, and wondered what thoughts – doubts even – were going through his mind at that moment.

My concentration during the departure of *Pendennis Castle* was broken by Martin Muncaster, who was at that time with Southern Television. "I'm afraid I've got a problem, Henry," he said, "I've left my gloves on board." My expression must have said to him, "We're watching an investment of millions of pounds sailing down the Solent and you're worrying about a pair of gloves," because he quickly added, "The trouble is they were given to me by my fiancee and she'll be furious!" I dutifully cabled the purser but he was unable to find them.

*Pendennis Castle's* departure received good coverage on the TV news programmes that night and in the press the next day. Subsequently, both *The Times* and the *Daily Telegraph* carried pictures of her arrival at Cape Town.

Happily, considerable interest had been aroused in the new flagship – indeed we had the world famous *Vogue* magazine devoting six whole pages to a special feature entitled, 'Cruising : the liner, the clothes', in their January 1959 issue, the nine photographs illustrating the feature having been taken on board *Pendennis Castle*, which received due credit.

This fashion link up subsequently resulted in the second outward voyage of the new mailship receiving as much publicity as the maiden voyage, for we were approached by Courtaulds-Celanese to stage fashion shows on board, or, as the London correspondent of the *East London Daily Despatch* put it: "The mailship run to South Africa gets a new glamourising – soft lights, music, and gorgeous model girls in wonderful clothes. When the *Pendennis Castle* sails from Southampton on 26 February 1959 High Fashion steps on board in the shape of London's top model girls."

The deal was that Courtaulds would provide a commentary, five models, 150 gowns, swim and leisure wear, and lingerie (all made entirely in Courtaulds-Celanese yarns and fabrics), whilst we would provide the accommodation and transport.

The Fashion Show was to be in the form of a three part revue – "Happy go lucky", "For leisure and pleasure" and "Round the clock" – all to be run by the well known London fashion commentator, Dorothy Fox. I found Dorothy Fox a delightfully competent person of great wit and charm, and a pleasure to work with. Indicative of her efficiency and experience was the exceptionally high quality of the team of five girls she chose.

She was naturally anxious to bring the team together as soon as possible, so accepted with alacrity the suggestion by deputy chair-

*The final line-up of the fashion shows on board "Pendennis Castle". The models are (From left to right) Stafford Hutchinson, Christina Gregg, Madeline Hobbs, Jean Clarke, and Sheila O'Hara.*
Phillips

*Top model Jean Clarke chats with commodore Mayhew at the Preview of the Fashion show held in Union-Castle's Old Bond Street Offices.*

*Sandra Paul*

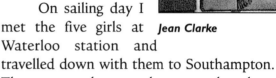

*Jean Clarke*

*Jean Clarke Sandra Paul*

man, Anthony Cayzer, that a preview show be held in London, particularly as in the new passenger booking offices in Old Bond Street we had the perfect venue – perfect in that guests could be received on the ground floor (the First Class booking hall) and the actual show could be carried out on the lower ground floor (the Tourist Class booking hall) which was reached by a sweeping curve of stairs from the floor above. Invitations went out to various Cayzer VIPs, contacts and friends, plus of course, press, both National and Trade. Although Wednesday, 18 February 1959 was a foggy night, a good audience had assembled by 6.30 pm and the ship's orchestra was playing merrily (amongst other songs "Thank heaven for little girls") and the chatter was bright and expectant.

The team of five girls for the preview had been increased by the the addition of the well-known model Sandra Paul, whose inclusion enabled Dorothy to show virtually every outfit to be displayed during the voyages and in Madeira. Today the glamourous Sandra is the wife of British Conservative Member of Parliament, Michael Howard, Leader of the Opposition in the House of Commons.

The whole show went off splendidly and was an undoubted success, auguring well for the programmes afloat in just over a week's time and at *Reid's Hotel*, Madeira, prior to return – and a repeat of the three reviews – aboard *Edinburgh Castle*.

On sailing day I met the five girls at Waterloo station and travelled down with them to Southampton. The press photographers caught them boarding the Boat Train and pictures appeared later that day in the London evening papers. Once on board *Pendennis Castle* the girls were persuaded to don swim and beachwear and parade on deck for a photo call. The passengers included Norman (now Sir Norman) Wisdom, who told me, that having read so much about it being fun to sail Union-Castle, he had decided this was for him. Naturally the photographers wanted to combine pictures of the little comedian with the five glamorous girls, who, incidentally, had already been photographed with Commodore Mayhew, the ship's Master, with his arms

*Comedian Norman Wisdom joins in the fun on board prior to the sailing of* **Pendennis Castle.**

Unfortunately, the *Edinburgh Castle* on the homeward run hit the most unpleasant weather in the Bay of Biscay and some of the girls were very unwell. But they proved real troopers and never missed a show.

The whole venture received the most satisfactory media coverage, and by mid 1959 *Pendennis Castle* was firmly established as the 'Funship' People were beginning to believe it was indeed fun to sail Union-Castle.

> Nearly forty years on I noted that ships in the Carnival Cruise Lines fleet plying between Florida and the Caribbean were being dubbed 'funships'.
>
> Three years later, scanning their latest brochure, I read to my surprise in the small print, that 'Funship' and 'Carnival's got the fun' are now registered trade marks of Carnival Cruise Lines!

around them. The pictures they took were either of Norman sitting on the ship's rail with girls cuddling up to him, or being carried by them as though about to be thrown overboard. At the end of all this frivolity deputy chairman Anthony Cayzer confessed to me that he had not had so much fun in a long time.

Arrival at Funchal, Madeira, was not without its problems in that one of the vast coffins (we all, from Dorothy Fox down, could find no better word for them) containing garments, slipped while being offloaded and fell, injuring one of the Portuguese dockers. Nevertheless, the shows at *Reid's* were a triumph, being reported in the local media most fully, with many pictures.

## Windsor Castle – 1960

To compensate to some extent for the disappointment following the last minute cancellation of the major shake down cruise, arrangements were made for a right royal send-off for Union-Castle's new flagship *Windsor Castle* on 18 August 1960. Once again, however, a threatened strike disrupted the elaborate preparations and the ship sailed from Southampton at 3 pm, an hour before her scheduled time.

Despite this inauspicious start, *Windsor Castle*, which was the largest vessel to ever make the Cape run regularly, proved a most popular ship, and during her seventeen years in service completed 124 round voyages to South Africa, carrying 270 000 passengers over 1 662 000 miles.◆

## CHAPTER SIX

# CAPTAINS & COMMODORES

Of the Captain, Commander, Master, or Skipper, whatever you prefer to call him, it can be truly said, in the words of President Truman, "The buck stops here." Resplendent he may appear with all his gold braid as he hosts the Captain's table, to which he regularly invites all the most attractive women on board. But if anything goes wrong, he and he alone, will carry the can.

It is with great pleasure I recall some of those gallant gentlemen I have known and admired.

## COMMODORE GEORGE MAYHEW

Many and varied are the responsibilities of the Captain of a great ocean going Liner, particularly when the accent is on FUN. At the time of the 1959 maiden voyage of the then flagship *Pendennis Castle*, Commodore George Mayhew, CBE, was photographed in the ship's gym with comedian Frankie Howard, in the Milk Bar with Dairy Princess Marion Crocker, and out on deck with three glamorous models – all part of his duties.

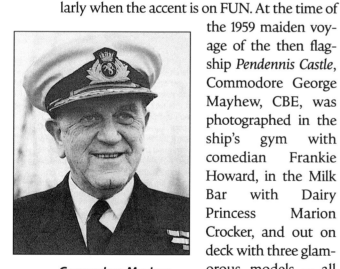

*Commodore Mayhew*

Born in 1901, George Henry Mayhew joined Union-Castle as a cadet in 1917. He received his first command in 1941. In 1943, when Master of the Company's fleet of refrigerated cargo vessels, his ship was sunk by a submarine torpedo off the Azores.

In 1950, now commanding passenger ships, Captain Mayhew pioneered the new one-class *Bloemfontein Castle*, and, a year later, was promoted to the mail service. 1953 was a notable year for Mayhew as not only did he take part in the Coronation Fleet Review, but he was also promoted Commodore. Six years later he introduced *Pendennis Castle* on New Year's day when he was awarded the CBE.

In 1960 he pioneered that 'Queen of the South Atlantic', *Windsor Castle*, leaving the sea the following year on appointment as Group Marine Superintendent for the British and Commonwealth Shipping Company, holding company for Union-Castle, Clan Line, King & Co. and King Line.

Commodore Mayhew's ever patient contribution in successfully publicising the three new vessels was invaluable. He could

*Captain Mayhew and Frankie Howard on a 'keep fit' gym horse. PA/Reuters*

*Captain Mayhew and Dairy Princess.* PA/Reuters

also be relied upon for a good quote or sound bite as it's known today. An excellent example of this was when he was faced on arrival at Southampton docks with no tugs because of a strike. Undaunted he manoeuvred his giant of over 28 000 tonnes, unaided, gently alongside the quay. At the press conference later, Mayhew announced triumphantly, "We never even cracked an egg shell." This marvellous quote did, of course, make all the papers.

My endearing memory, apart from all the ready help he gave me in putting over the FUN message, was during a voyage from Madeira, homeward bound for Southampton.

*Captain Mayhew with three glamourous models.*
Planet News

Among the passengers was former Gaiety Girl, Ruby Miller, 'toast of the stage door Johnnies and a dancing partner of Edward VII', as she was remembered in the media on her death in 1976 at the age of eighty-six. At the gala dance the night before docking, Miss Miller was persuaded to sing for us by Commodore Mayhew. It was a magic moment as Ruby sang, 'You are my honey, honey, I am the bee', with the gallant Commodore accompanying her on the piano.

## CAPTAIN JOHN FISHER

Captain John Fisher was the long-time Commander of the mailship *Pretoria Castle*. John Douglas Ben Fisher had originally joined Union-Castle as a Fourth Officer in 1929. During the war he was a commodore navigator in troop convoys.

A Freeman of the City of London, his hobbies were, golf, cricket, writing, horseracing, and – although he did not list it – fun. Indeed, since his first mailship command he had built up quite a reputation for himself as 'the man it was fun to sail with', be it as M.C. at the ship's dances, running the tombola (shipboard name for Bingo), captaining the officers' cricket team, doing the commentary for one of

*Captain John Fisher*

his own colour films of a voyage to South Africa, or singing saucy songs accompanying himself on the ukelele.

Perhaps all this exuberance was a natural reaction to Sir Vernon Thomson's austerity, for Captain Fisher used to tell how as a junior officer, when there was a fixed time for public rooms on Company ships to close, he used to go in and say, "I'm sorry, but lights have to be turned out now", and switch them off, leaving laggards to stumble out in the dark.

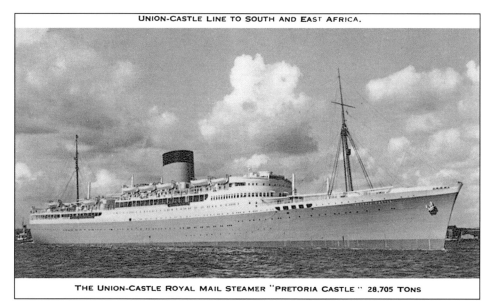

UNION-CASTLE LINE TO SOUTH AND EAST AFRICA.

THE UNION-CASTLE ROYAL MAIL STEAMER "PRETORIA CASTLE" 28,705 TONS

John Fisher was, above all, a teller of stories – 'a reckless raconteur' was the delightful description afforded him by one journalist. He worked on the principle that if he reeled off a dozen stories, at least one should make you laugh. My favourite Captain Fisher anecdote concerned the retired Colonel who loved show jumping, which I heard during a voyage to the Cape. When *Pretoria Castle* was in Cape Town he invited the Colonel to a show jumping event. One of the entrants was a top executive of O.K. Bazaars, South Africa's equivalent of British Home Stores. An enthusiastic and

ardent supporter of the sport, this gentleman's skill in the saddle in no way matched his love for the sport. So, to quote Fisher's own words, "He was lolloping round the ring like a sack of potatoes," which prompted the Colonel to ask, "Who the hell's that?" Captain Fisher told him. "Who?" roared the Colonel, who was somewhat deaf. "Mr. X, Sir, OK Bazaars," repeated Fisher. "Eighth Hussars," thundered the Colonel. "The man ought to be bloody well shot!"

The theme 'It's fun to sail Union-Castle' was obviously very much in the mind of deputy chairman Anthony Cayzer when he took John Fisher off *Pretoria Castle* to Command the *Rhodesia Castle* during her two ten day cruises in 1958. Undoubtedly, the sheer weight of his personality set the seal on the success of these special voyages.

One of the journalists aboard , the late Alison Adburgham, wrote: "Tacking about the lounge and decks, distributing the largesse of his personality with here a word

THE SPECULATION in shipping circles in 1983 that Safmarine were considering resuming the Cape Run (which Union-Castle had terminated six years earlier) proved correct when they purchased the 18 834grt West German cruise ship *Astor*, announcing a regular service would commence in early 1984. The Master of the luxury liner was Commodore Ivan Currie. I asked him if he was related to the great Sir Donald of that name. He laughed and said, "I wish I was." Now that would have been a story.

*Commodore Currie (2nd from Left) and officers of SAFMarine's Astor.*

**SA Vaal**

and there a nod, Captain Fisher not only enjoyed himself, but was seen to be enjoying himself. That the Captain should be seen enjoying himself is vital," she added, "As it is from him that the passengers take their cue." "Nevertheless," she concluded, "His easy affability was tempered by a brisk seaworthiness. Even when he was dancing with castanets at three o'clock in the morning he gave the impression that his spiritual home was on the navigation bridge."

When I joined Union-Castle as a junior clerk, I was first sent to the Company's London Docks office, where, from time to time, I went aboard ships to assist paying the crew. On one occasion, three of the men started arguing among themselves, an argument that became so heated that the Captain eventually rose from the paying-out table and addressed these husky seamen thus: "Now you're all being very naughty, so Mr. Damant and I are going aloft to my cabin for five minutes so that you can settle down." It worked like a charm.

Then there was Captain JC Brown whose initials were apt in that, like so many seamen, he was deeply religious. Again, like so many seamen, he had a proud war record.

Asked by a woman passenger if he had been afraid when the bombs were falling, he replied, "No, Madam; I knew I was safe in the arms of Jesus."

If a passenger is discovered missing, the Captain has no option but to turn his ship around and retrace the exact route back to the last port of call. In September 1970 an inebriated gentleman joined the luxury Blue Train in Johannesburg and remained in that state for the whole of the journey to Cape Town, where, to the dismay of his fellow passengers, he went on board *SA Vaal* (formerly *Transvaal Castle* prior to her being sold to Safmarine) by which they were booked for the journey to Southampton.

He continued imbibing once they were at sea and subsequently fell overboard. His disappearance was not noticed for some while, but when it was, Captain Alan Freer plotted a search area sixty miles long and after some eleven and a half hours the missing passenger was spotted only eighty yards off the original course! It was thought the amount of alcohol in his system prevented his dying of exposure, although he was badly blistered by the sun and the elements. He was hailed by the media as 'The luckiest man alive', although the man himself, who was known to be a good swimmer, reckoned, "There was a good chance I was going to be rescued, so I bashed on."

The disappearance of a sixty-four year old housewife aboard *Windsor Castle* bound for the Cape was not discovered for over an hour. After a thorough search on board Captain Patrick Beadon ordered the ship to turn about. The liner retraced her path – aided by the occasional sighting of normal discarded rubbish that had not yet sunk. Just twenty minutes after turning she was sighted, swimming strongly. The lady was hoisted aboard and spent the rest of her voyage to Port Elizabeth in the ship' s hospital recovering from the shock. Captain Beadon considered the chances of finding her were a million to one. Cost to the company was well over £4000.

Finally, spare a thought for the unfortunate captain of the *Durban Castle* whose passenger list included a Miss Gaye Gibson and crew list a steward named James Camb. When the ship arrived in the London docks Camb was arrested and charged with the murder of twenty-one year old actress Gaye Gibson by pushing her through the porthole of her cabin into the ocean. The prosecution alleged he had raped and then strangled her. Her body was never recovered and the case was certainly unusual – a murder trial and conviction without a body.

Sadly, such being the way of things, Union-Castle at the time received maximum national media coverage, not from the then triumphant Phoenix-like emergence of her fleet to pre-war splendour, but from this sordid incident. Over the years that followed every time a popular newspaper, usually a Sunday, announced a series of famous murder cases, this was the first to be featured. For a long time after, on being introduced at parties, receptions, and the like, I had to learn to live with the response: "Union-Castle eh! That's the Line that pushes its female passengers through the porthole, isn't it?"

Incidentally, a few months after the Gaye Gibson affair the good ship *Durban Castle* carried out a dramatic rescue at sea. All the papers carried the story, but one popular daily could not resist headlining their report, 'Murder ship sails to the rescue'. Needless to say since, 'The buck stops here', the captain of the *Durban Castle* had been sacked and the new skipper received the accolades for the rescue.◆

**Windsor Castle** *leaving Cape Town for the last time.*

LET THE INIMITABLE Captain John Fisher have the last word …

Two days after *Rhodesia Castle* left Tilbury on the first of the two 1958 cruises, Paul Tanfield's diary in *The Daily Mail* contained and amusing tailpiece. Headed 'Snob, snob' it read: "Captain John Fisher, of the Union-Castle liner *Rhodesia Castle* was still laughing yesterday after a snub from one of his cruise passengers. 'I asked the man if he would like to join me for his meals at the captain's table, to which he replied, 'What? Me sit with the crew when I've paid all this money to go on a cruise … not bloody likely!'"

**Captain John Fisher welcoming guests to the Captain's Cocktail Party.** *Union-Castle*

## CHAPTER SEVEN

# EVERY THURSDAY AT 4 O'CLOCK

Southampton's fine Civic Centre boasts a splendid clock tower, from which the striking of certain hours is preceded by a peal of bells playing the melody of 'Oh God our help in ages past.' For many years the first stroke of four o'clock on a Thursday afternoon following Isaac Watt's well loved hymn would be answered by a deep throated blast of the siren of one of the fleet of eight Union-Castle mailships which each week, month in and month out, would then pull away from the berth in Southampton Docks and head south to the sun for Cape Town.

And every Friday, soon after sunrise, during this exciting period, another great Castle liner would dock at Southampton, loaded with passengers, cargo, and mail.

> In 1891 the Castle Line chose Southampton as their port of departure for the Cape, and with Sir Donald Currie's customary flair for publicity, the new service was inaugurated by the Line's flagship, *Dunotar Castle*.
>
> In a speech on sailing day Sir Donald said, "This is the beginning of an era in the history of Southampton."
>
> How right he was. Following the amalgamation in 1900 of the Union and Castle Lines, the port of Southampton was firmly established as the base for the mailship and remained so for the next seventy-seven years.

It was said that people at the Cape set their watches by the arrival of the mailship, just as the people of Southampton, hearing that siren blast from the docks on a Thursday, knew it was 4 pm precisely.

The regularity of this unique service owed much to Southampton's natural advantages, most important of which is the rare phenomenon of two high tides in every twenty four hours and the shelter provided by the Isle of Wight. As such, it was the perfect big ship port and was used extensively in the fifties and sixties by most of the world's finest liners.

The North Atlantic Trade was then booming with an average of thirty-five sailings a month. Great ships such as the *Queens*, the *France*, the *United States*, and many more regularly graced the port. But it was the Castle boats, as they were fondly, albeit inaccurately referred to locally, that consistently made the news with their unique clockwork-like service in and out of Southampton.

Fifty years ago the Port of Southampton had a very large press corps of both reporters and photographers, many of

**DOYEN OF THE SHIPPING REPORTERS,** Jack Frost, MBE, had been in Fleet Street fifty-two years when he retired in 1965. He started as a messenger in *The Daily Mail* tape room and since then had worked at every job for just about every past and present daily, with a few 'Sundays' and magazines thrown in.

Since 1938, when he joined *The Daily Telegraph*, he had travelled the world as shipping correspondent. Religiously, every May the first, he donned a straw boater, which he continued to wear until October the first. Right from the start, when I was appointed press officer, Jack Frost was of very great help to me and I shall always remember him with great affection.

*The author's wife, Linda Damant, enjoying a joke with Jack Frost on board at Southampton.*

whom would join me for lunch on board the outgoing vessel on Thursday and for breakfast on the incoming vessel the next day.

The then nine nationals, which included now defunct newspapers such as *The Daily Herald*, *Daily Sketch*, and *News Chronicle*, all had shipping correspondents, as did the London evening papers, the *News* and *Standard*.

Those Fleet Street based journalists, headed up by the *Telegraph's* Jack Frost, normally only appeared at the port on special occasions, but all had a local representative covering for them. In addition *Argus South Africa Newspapers* had their local man, whilst BBC, Southampton, was represented by Ron Allison (later to become press secretary at Buckingham Palace) and there was also the newly started Southern Television. Last, but certainly not least, there was Arthur Taylor, shipping reporter for the Southampton based *Southern Evening Echo*, who wrote a daily 'Round the Port' column.

As I have already indicated, I was delighted to be appointed chief press and public relations officer for the British and Commonwealth Shipping Group, which embraced the Clan Line, Houston Line, King Line, Natal Line, Scottish Shire Line, Scottish Tankers and Union-Castle Line. The bulk of my duties in this capacity continued to be media relations and the necessity for this responsibility was highlighted just before the merger when one of the Line's 'Round Africa' ships damaged a propeller severely and limped into Gibraltar to wait for a replacement to be flown out and fitted.

News of the mishap reached the *Daily Express* which received the customary response to their request for fuller details – "No comment". This policy – if you could call it such – was based presumably on the premise of 'Least said, soonest mended.' It was a policy, however, that became seriously unstuck in the matter of 'The broken propeller.'

The frustrated reporter went to the files where he found the vessel in question had, over the years, suffered a number of breakdowns. The next day there appeared a full length column, complete with picture, in the centre of the middle page and headlined, 'This unfortunate ship!'

Had we been frank and open with them, I reckon we would have been unlucky if the incident had been covered in more than three lines – if at all. The way I saw it was that the press had a job to do. If I could make this job as easy as possible for them, this would be to the advantage of us both. Furthermore, I must always tell them the truth and I must trust them, even to the extent of 'off the record' taking them into my complete confidence. Once they had learned to trust me, my task would become that much easier. Finally, although I might succeed in establishing the closest possible relationship with them, I must never expect the press to 'hide', 'conceal' or 'bury' (as the current phrases go), a genuine piece of bad news. It was their job to report it and it would be churlish of me to expect them to do otherwise. The late Ed Murrow best summed it up when, as Director of the US Information Agency, he said: "The only thing to do as far as foreign correspondents are concerned is to give them maximum facilities and access to the maximum amount of information. What they write is their own affair."

But, whilst it was always my aim to give the media whatsoever they wanted as regards interviews, pictures, etc., at the same time when dealing with the company's passengers, I had a positive duty to ensure that in no way they be pestered, pursued or upset.

Very early on in my career as Press Officer, I was to be faced with such a situation. One picture, it is said, is worth a thousand words, which no doubt accounted for the fact that in those halcyon days of the 1950s the port of Southampton, in addition to reporters, boasted a large number of press photographers. They could prove quite a handful as, for example, when a contingent of South African scouts, guides, cubs and brownies arrived early on Friday morning to attend the World Jamboree.

Their leader was a rotund, bespectacled man of about fifty who posed cheerfully with two attractive young cub mistresses the photographers had cleverly rounded up. A request from one of them for him to kiss them not unnaturally met with some resistance. Then, when scuffling broke out among the cameramen, one of whom accused another of hogging his patch, the Chief Scout decided he had had enough. I quickly followed him back to his cabin to apologise on behalf of the photographers who, I suggested, must have been carried away with enthusiasm. He was somewhat tense, but eventually accepted the apologies.

On return to the office I wrote to the photographers concerned, pointing out they came on board the Union-Castle ships as guests at our invitation and, consequently, I expected them to act accordingly. I finished by saying that should there be any further such incidents, I would, without hesitation, withdraw their Press passes. By return I received written apologies from them all and wrote back to them saying that the incident was now forgotten.

Travel by sea was then so very much in vogue, with the famous, week by week, departing from and arriving at Southampton. Because of this, and also to cope with such problems as might arise following the introduction of the three big liners into the mail service, Sir Nicholas Cayzer created a new appointment – Southampton Area Manager for Union-Castle Line. The post was filled by Major-General George Erroll Prior-Palmer, CB, DSO, Legion of Honour, Croix de Guerre avec Palme.

Such things, it seems, never change. Reports from Cape Town in March 1997 covering the meeting of the late Diana, Princess of Wales, with President Nelson Mandela, told how requests from photographers for him to kiss the Princess were declined, "with embarrassed smiles from both."

Headlining his story 'Little ship General switches to liners' the *Daily Express* shipping man, Montague Lacey, wrote: "The man who led the first little boats and amphibious vehicles on to the Normandy beaches on D-Day gets a new job today with the Big Ships." He is probably best remembered today as the justly proud father of top rider and show jumper Lucinda Green. General Prior-Palmer was a man for whom I quickly gained very great respect and, as we shall see later, he was on occasion to get me out of a most terrible fix, for which I remain ever grateful.

The camaraderie amongst the journalists was impressive. Sometimes one of them would arrive late to find the VIP he was interested in had already been interviewed by others, who always made no bones about filling in the details for him.

All in all, it was a most fascinating period with interest in the Union-Castle Line at its height, and I shall always be grateful to those at Southampton who played so major a part in helping me to create such interest.

One of the banes of my press relation's life was the stowaway. Not so much at Southampton but mainly at Cape Town where security was so lax it was the easiest thing in the world to go aboard the northbound mailship on sailing day and remain undiscovered until the ship was well out at sea. With ten days ahead before reaching Las Palmas or Madeira, where neither the Spanish nor the Portuguese wanted to know, stowaways invariably made Southampton, where the Press unfortunately tended to treat them as heroes. This treatment, not unnaturally, encouraged others to stowaway.

Then someone came up with the solution. At one stage in every voyage mailships crossed on their way to and from South Africa, always an occasion for cheers and waves accompanied by the sounding of the ship's sirens, so it was decided in future to transfer stowaways in mid ocean – an additional source of entertainment for the pas-

**57**

sengers. So, after only a few days, culprits found themselves back in Cape Town and this procedure helped to curtail the nuisance they caused.

But the arrangements did not always work. On the last round voyage of the Union-Castle flagship *Windsor Castle* in September 1977 no less than two stowaways virtually got away with it. The first was a South African journalist whose work permit had run out in Britain. He was keen to get home but nevertheless gave himself up a few hours out of Southampton. However the passengers had a whip round and raised the £350 single fare for him to repay in South Africa.

The second offender, an eighteen year old from Stevenage, was not so lucky. Throughout the 13 190 mile haul from Britain to South Africa and back he was kept in the crew's quarters and not allowed to fraternise with the fare-paying passengers. He was first off *Windsor Castle* when she finally docked at Southampton.

Another of my problems was the 'Pretty girl.' Beauty queens, entertainers, dancers, models, and sometimes just pretty girl passengers, were always sought out by the photographic corps at Southampton. The cameraman had but one way of posing them for pictures – seated on the ship's rail, waving and with their legs crossed. If they took their picture from a semi kneeling position, they did, of course, get an attractive glimpse of thigh. On more than one occasion I was instructed by the powers that be that I must not let girls pose in this way – not because of their legs, but fear that they would fall overboard.

Considerable interest was aroused in March 1959 by Union-Castle's decision to appoint female purser's clerks – quickly dubbed purserettes. The first to arrive from

*Comedian Sir Norman Wisdom perched with the **Pendennis Castle** model girls on a ship's rail - but not one with the sea behind! Planet News*

OCTOBER 1958 saw the election of eighteen year old 'Miss South Africa', Penelope Coelen as 'Miss World'. *The Daily Sketch* waxed lyrical about her success. "Penny," they wrote, "was the first of the international beauties to arrive here for the contest. And she was in the lead all the way – one of the most popular winners of the title in recent years. As soon as she appeared last night the *Lyceum* audience gave her a big round of applause."

We always tried to be alert to worthwhile opportunities for obtaining publicity for the Line, so the chairman agreed to my offering Penny Coelen a job in the PR Department. A week or so later the commissionaire at front reception rang up to say there was a Miss Coelen to see me about a letter I had written to her. Sadly, the most beautiful girl in the world – for 1958/9 anyway – had come to turn down the offer."

**Penelope Coelen.** *South Africa House*

South Africa was Suzette Pienaar, who, looking attractively smart in her uniform, was duly photographed – not sitting on the ship's rail. The photograph featured that evening on the front pages of both the *London Evening News* and the *Evening Standard*. Such is the attraction to the media of the 'pretty girl' that on the same afternoon Central Press Photos asked if they could photograph Suzette "under instruction" at the Line's head office. One of the resultant pictures of her with Marine Superintendent Captain Elvish actually made *The Times*.

Then, Kemsley Newspapers interviewed her, Sport & General Press Agency photographed her; the London-based South African Press interviewed her and, finally, PA/Reuter Photos took pictures of her as she left on her first assignment in April 1959. So Suzette Pienaar was a very busy girl and played an important part in our publicity programme at the time.

'Damage Limitation is one of those catch phrases which probably originated in

the United States. Two examples occurred when, in 1958, the decision to go cruising was announced.

At the suggestion of our advertising agents, the two sailings were dubbed "friendship cruises", a name which caused the *Sunday Pictorial* a considerable degree of curiosity and, indeed, suspicion. "Could they," they said, "discuss the matter with me? At lunchtime? At El Vinos?" I arrived at the famous Fleet Street wine bar to find the paper's news editor, together with someone from picture features and a staff reporter, all awaiting me.

Introductions over, pleasantries exchanged, and drinks ordered, the news editor then turned to me and said: "Henry, these...er... friendship cruises; what can you tell us about them?" I recited dates, ports of call, and fares. "Yes, yes," he said, "but why ..." – at this point he paused and I expected him to glance clandestinely over his shoulder, but he didn't – "... why, friendship cruises?" with heavy emphasis on the somewhat innocent word 'friendship'. The penny was beginning to drop. Quite obviously they thought they had uncovered something sinister and were conjuring up visions of some dubious dating agency afloat! "Look," I said, "if you gentlemen would like to go on one of these cruises I can easily arrange." "No, no," said the news editor, somewhat stiffly, "If the *Pictorial* travels it pays its own fare." I heard no more.

To help promote the cruises we arranged for two free passages to be the Star prize on the popular *Take your pick* TV quiz. The prize was won by Mrs. Rosalind Green, who was young, pretty, and had only been married a few months. So delighted was she at winning, she threw her arms around a surprised Michael Miles, the quizmaster, and wept for joy.

But, sadly, the next day she phoned me to say she could not accept the prize. Rosalind explained she and her husband were saving hard to put down a deposit on a

*'Friendship Cruises' Pamphlet.*

house – money they thought they would have to dip into to buy new clothes, if they accepted the cruise. "We'll probably regret it for the rest of our lives," she added. "Leave it to me," I said, "I'll ring you back shortly."

I reported the situation to the chairman, who, after a few seconds of thought, said: "Right, this is what we do. All shore excursions will be free for them both. There will be a bottle of wine with the compliments of the company for them at dinner each evening. And arrange for an *ex gratia* payment to be made to them for clothes, etc." How did they get on? Let Jack Frost, who was on the same cruise, take up the story. Describing the cruise as, "One of the friendliest voyages I have known in thirty years," he reported that this spirit of friendship, "made a great difference to the enjoyment of a young Fulham couple, Richard Green, an engineer, twenty-one, and his wife, Rosalind, nineteen, a telephonist. They were diffident about coming, asked for a table on their own, and were apprehensive about the attitude of seasoned cruisers to them." They need not have worried. They were asked to join other people and soon put at their ease. And for the four month anniversary of their marriage, Chief Steward White arranged a wedding cake. Indeed, as I realised when I met them when the ship docked at Southampton , Mr and Mrs Green were being thoroughly spoilt by sundry 'uncles' and 'aunts'. Damage limitation, and PR, at its very best.◆

*Quizmaster Michael Miles with Richard and Rosalind Green.*

## CHAPTER EIGHT

# SOME MEMORABLE PASSENGERS

### SIR WINSTON CHURCHILL

At the turn of the century, Winston Churchill, as Boer War correspondent for the *London Morning Post*, sailed by Union-Castle to Cape Town, where he stayed at the *Mount Nelson Hotel*, which he found, "A most excellent and well appointed establishment which may be thoroughly appreciated after a sea voyage."

Fifty years later, Churchill travelled Union-Castle again, but this time only as far as Madeira, where he went to paint, staying, of course, at *Reid's Hotel*. The four o'clock Thursday departure was now legendary, but on this occasion the mailship had to wait one hour for Sir Winston to board. "One legend to another," as someone wrote at the time.

At the end of the return voyage Churchill was obviously keen to disembark and was out on the deck by the gangway almost as soon as it was down. The Captain and officers had hastily assembled to see him off and one keen young type noticed that the great man had the pillow from his bunk under his arm. Stepping forward, he saluted smartly and said, "I'll relieve you of that, Sir." Churchill turned, looked the young

*Sir Winston Churchill www.churchillonline.org.uk*

officer straight in the eye, and growled, "Over my dead body young man; that's the most comfortable pillow I've ever slept on." And he stomped ashore with it.

### FIELD MARSHALL
### VISCOUNT MONTGOMERY OF ALAMEIN

The tricky passenger/press relationship proved a real cliffhanger in the case of the legendary Monty who had gone to South Africa in November 1959, at the expense of the *Sunday Times*, for which he was to write a report on the country.

Once it was known he was on his way home, I was inundated with requests from Press, Radio, and TV for passes to go aboard the mailship on arrival at Southampton and to interview him. In addition to the Southampton Press Corps, who had already stated their intention to be there to a man, there were London based journalists on the nationals and from South African newspapers, plus broadcasting and television representatives, all wishing to be there.

Good manners dictated I should cable Montgomery at Las Palmas, the vessel's last port of call, to get approval to his holding a Press Conference in the First Class library at eight o'clock on the Friday morning the ship docked. I received his reply by return. It contained but one word – "No." On the Thursday night it was, I felt, a ludicrous situation, sitting there at the Polygon Hotel bar discussing the Press Conference with the large contingent down from London and that cable in my pocket. The next morning I had successfully ushered all the Pressmen into the library by ten-to-eight and was standing in the main foyer debating whether to go back and tell them it was all off, or to throw myself on the mercy of Montgomery (Old soldier, job at stake that sort of thing) when Major General Prior-Palmer arrived on board.

*The author and Field Marshall Viscount Montgomery of Alamein.* Phillips

"You're looking fed up, Damant," he said, "What's up?" I told him. "That man was responsible for my having to land on the Normandy beaches in June '44," the General declared. "He owes me a favour." Whereupon he strode away. After what seemed an age he returned – with Montgomery. He introduced me. In that distinctive voice Monty said, "So you look after the Press eh? I don't envy you your job." So saying he marched into the library where he gave a splendid press conference.

The photograph shows a smiling Montgomery, having just cracked a joke, surrounded by laughing journalists and photographers, with me at his side, laughing somewhat hysterically. It had, after all, been one of those mornings!

## GLYNIS JOHNS

A similar situation arose here. I was most interested to learn that the delicious Glynis, one of my favourite actresses, was to sail Union-Castle at the end of 1958. She was photographed, prior to departure, at Waterloo station and the caption read: "Glynis Johns, the film actress, leaves Waterloo on the *Edinburgh Castle* boat train with her mother for South Africa where they will spend Christmas with relations whom they have not seen for twenty-five years." With freckled face and big bright eyes, she looked extremely pretty, but there was sad-

ness behind her smile. Her second marriage had just broken up.

During the journey down to Southampton docks I looked in on them and Glynis's father, the veteran actor Melvyn Johns, quickly steered me out into the corridor. In his rich Welsh voice he told me that his daughter was very low and, indeed, felt that there must be something wrong with her in that, for the second time her marriage had broken up. He asked me to protect her from the press at Southampton, and I promised to do my best.

The journalists and photographers awaiting me on board *Edinburgh Castle* were, naturally, eager to see Glynis Johns. Here, again, was the tightrope situation. On the one hand I must not allow a passenger to be

*Glynis Johns, the film actress, leaves Waterloo, on the* **Edinburgh Castle** *boat train with her mother, for South Africa where they will spend Christmas with relations whom they have not seen for twenty-five years.* Sport & General

subjected to a grilling from the media. On the other hand it was also my job to try and give the media what they wanted. I explained her present feelings to them but they were adamant. With some reluctance I agreed to approach her. Glynis was all alone in her cabin, looking wistfully attractive, utterly feminine, and much in need of protection.

In that famous tiny voice of hers, she asked to be excused the suggested interview. I'm afraid I gently persisted and eventually she agreed to see the Press on my personal assurance that they would not be too hard on her.

As we entered the First Class Smoke Room with the Press Corps gathered in the far corner, Glynis gripped my arm very hard as we made our seemingly endless way towards them. To their eternal credit the gentlemen of the Press proved themselves gentlemen indeed and I returned a relieved Glynis Johns to her cabin with honour satisfied on both sides.

## TOMMY STEELE

No such problem here.

The later fifties saw the emergence on the entertainment world of the Pop Star. Each week, or so it seemed, some new idol was foisted on to the public, the teenage section of whom welcomed them, literally, with open arms. After a brief spell as 'Top of the Pops', the vast majority vanished never to be seen or heard of again.

One of the exceptions to this was 'The Cockney kid from Bermondsey', Tommy Steele, described in those days as a Rock and Roll singer. He was subsequently to be recognised as an entertainer of some talent.

In February 1958 it was decided that Tommy should make a 'variety tour' of South Africa, and I accompanied him on the Boat Train to Southampton. His two managers, Larry Parnes and John Kennedy, travelled down with us and talked of nothing but various deals they were hoping to bring off, subject to Steele's approval. He showed little interest in anything they put forward.

**Tommy Steele** *Planet News*

Actually he did not look very well. He was pale, had a bad skin, and every now and then, blinked his eyes rapidly in what I assumed was some sort of nervous tic.

I left them to their business discussions after a while and was almost immediately buttonholed by Captain Elvish who was in the next compartment. Tall and bluff, Elvish, a former Clan Line skipper, was the group's marine superintendent. "What's Steele like?" he asked. "He's OK, I said, but see for yourself." I took him next door and introduced him. The fact that Steele had once been a merchant seaman and was now a pop idol no doubt intrigued Captain Elvish, who eventually returned with the comment, "He's quite a nice lad." I gathered the impression that he had reached this conclusion with some surprise.

At the ship's side a giggle of young girls greeted Steele with screams, shrieks, and squeals of delight, but he succeeded in getting on board unscathed. On his return some weeks later there was a full complement of pressmen and photographers to interview and photograph him. Tommy said the one thing he was looking forward to was a meat pie with green pea sauce. He had brought a great number of souvenirs with him, including an assegai (spear) and shield, which he brandished on deck to the delight of the photographers. One of the shots made the *London Evening News* that day.

He had brought presents for all the family, which he displayed eagerly to the press. He was especially fond of a mechanical car, which was for his young brother and which he ran, repeatedly, up and down the ship's library.

Tommy Steele looked considerably healthier. His skin was clearer and suntanned, and he did not blink so disconcertingly every now and then. In short, the perfect advertisement for a sea voyage – especially one by Union-Castle – on which to rest, relax, and recuperate.

## ANNE HEYWOOD

Typical of the Cayzer's flair was their decision to go cruising in 1958 – something that Union-Castle had not done in many a year. The possibility of doing so arose out of the rescheduling of the 'Round Africa' service that would have resulted in the *Rhodesia Castle* being idle for some weeks. Laying up a ship for any length of time is a costly business. Far better to employ her, especially at this time when by cruising we could further the idea that it was "Fun to travel Union-Castle."

This was obviously very much in the mind of Deputy Chairmen Anthony Cayzer when he summed up a meeting to discuss promotional activities and publicity for the two cruises by proclaiming: "What we want is film stars – pretty girls – lots of fun!"

At the time of the cruises Britain's great movie mogul was J. Arthur Rank, and a call to his Mayfair offices put me in touch with one of his publicity men, Tony Hill, to whom I explained the situation. He said he would look at their production schedules

*Film Actress, Anne Haywood with huge bouquet of flowers before embarking on* **Rhodesia Castle.** *Poppofoto (UP)*

and let me know who were free during the period of the second cruise. He reported back that only one actress was available at that time – Anne Heywood. The deal was that she, Hill, and photographer Cornel Lucas would all travel free on the cruise, in return for which the Rank publicity machine would obtain for us maximum coverage for the voyage. Tony Hill flooded us with studio portraits and career details, and the deal was approved.

Anne Heywood had started her film career two years earlier and was under contract to the Rank Organisation. Prior to this she had won several beauty contests including the title of 'Miss Britain.' At the age of eighteen she was touring music halls with the Carroll Lewis talent discovery show. All this she had done under her real name of Violet Pretty. Here follows a fan letter from me:

I met Anne Heywood at Waterloo to travel down to Southampton on the Boat Train. One of the blurbs issued by the Rank Artiste Publicity Department said of her under the heading "Appearance – Hair: dark brown. Eyes: grey/green. Weight: 8 st. 12 lbs. (124 lbs). Height: 5ft. 5ins. Bust: 36. Waist: 23. Hips: 36. To which I would have added – elegant and beautiful. She was wearing a pale cream coloured jacket and skirt and looked deliciously cool.

After a while I ordered coffee. Suddenly Anne tipped her cup over her jacket. I knew that once we arrived at the ship's side, the photographers would be waiting, so if Anne had screamed, sworn, ranted and raved, or even had a fit of the vapours I would have understood. She did none of these things. She calmly removed her jacket, dabbed at the stain with a dampened serviette and hung it up to dry. My admiration knew no bounds.

A large bouquet of flowers was presented to Anne at the foot of the gangway and the cameramen snapped away. One result was a delightful six inch by four inch picture of Anne, the flowers carefully hiding the coffee stain, on the front page of the *Daily Mirror* next day. Below the headline. 'Anne sails off on a "Friendship Cruise," the caption read: "British film star Anne Heywood hugs a bunch of flowers as she boards the *Rhodesia Castle* at Southampton yesterday for what the shipping line calls a 'Ten day Friendship Cruise'. The liner will call at Gibraltar, Malaga in Spain, Casablanca, and Lisbon." We could not have done better had we been invited to write it ourselves.

I lunched with Anne at the Captain's table that was presided over by Anthony Cayzer, Captain Fisher being about his duties elsewhere. Anne Heywood is what I believe the Scots call a bonny talker and the conversation flowed. She spoke freely and frankly about her background and upbringing. Certainly she had come up the hard way. She was justly proud of what she had achieved so far, but, equally, was determined to succeed further. But Anne did not talk just of herself. We even discussed my redecorating the kitchen during the following week that I was taking off as part of my annual leave.

---

**"LETTER FROM ANOTHER FAN"**

For the past ten years I have contributed a column on travel to South Africa and on Cape wines, laced with some nostalgia, to *South Africa News*, in which, in November 1996, I wrote about Anne Heywood.

This inspired Mr. Geoffrey Cant , who was living in a home for the disabled Yorkshire, to write an excited letter to me. "I just knew whose picture it was before reading the caption," he wrote, "and my heart leapt with a moment of joy. You see," he explained, "I was there as one of the three regular carpenters on the *Rhodesia Castle*." Apparently, one morning, he was sent to Anne Heywood's cabin to carry out certain work.

"She was," he recalled, "a very beautiful young lady. She was very chatty and wanted to know what else I did on the ship, where I had been on other ships, etc. Then," he continued, "she rang for the stewardess and ordered coffee for two. She was quite content to sit with me and chat for a while. I am now nearing sixty but at that time I was twenty-one years old," wrote Geoffrey Cant, "and I fell in love with her there and then!"

He concluded his charming letter to me by saying that he was going to paste my article on a stiff piece of cardboard and hang it on his wall.

It was a memorable meal and was obviously enjoyed by the Deputy Chairman who had an eye for a pretty girl – and why not? With a laugh he said to me, "Anne reminds me of my mother-in-law!" Explanation: Anthony Cayzer married the elder daughter of Lord Oranmore and Browne, who subsequently remarried – the blonde and leggy actress Sally Grey.

The mighty Rank organisation kept its word with us and achieved some excellent publicity for us, including a massive twelve by nine inch picture of Anne in one of the national newspapers.

It was now time for me to welcome the ship back to Tilbury, so, putting aside my paintbrush and closing the door on the kitchen, I drove down to the docks. Having made myself known to Captain Fisher and checked for any Pressmen, I then sought out Anne Heywood. She was in her cabin, looking sun tanned and gorgeous. "Hello Henry," she said, "How's the kitchen going?" A star indeed and a very lovely lady.

*Denis Compton signs the Visitors Book at South Africa House under the watchful eye of Ambassador Dr. Carel de Wet. Keystone Press*

## DENIS COMPTON

I first met Denis in the fifties on his return from a visit to South Africa when I hoped to arrange for the Press Corps to interview him and take pictures.

The incoming mailships docked at Southampton promptly at 6 am on Fridays. This was not as drastic as it sounds, as passengers were allowed to indulge in full English breakfasts before disembarking.

I espied Denis breakfasting alone and on finishing I accosted him to ask if he and his South African wife Valerie would be prepared to be photographed with their two children. "Of course, old boy" he said, "Let's go to the cabin." Ever patient Denis posed this way and that, but I'm afraid the lovely Valerie found it all a bit of a bore.

Denis Compton had the reputation of being late and unreliable. I agree with the former but not the latter.

When the South African cricketers toured England in the 1960s it was decided to run a Cape Wine Awards promotion, the scheme being launched at a party at South Africa House. Many well-known cricketers, including Compton, were invited to attend.

"He won't come," people said to me, but with the reception twenty minutes under way, I was told there was a phone call for me. It was Denis. "Just coming off the motorway. I'll be with you in a quarter of an hour." And he was. Having signed in he whispered to me, "Do you think I could have a whisky?" Of course he could.

Later that season, in the Middlesex match at Lords against the tourists, twenty-one year old Clive Radley made his maiden century and had the added satisfaction of sharing in a record sixth wicket stand with his skipper, Fred Titmus, who also scored a hundred. I had asked Denis if he would present cases of South African wine to Radley and Titmus in the dressing room at the tea interval. "He won't remember," people said to me.Up in the stand I could see him seated with his wife. As the players left the field for tea he got up and made his way towards me. "Just coming, old boy," he said.

Denis Compton was a charmingly modest man who, together with Bill Edrich, totally dominated the series against South Africa in England in 1947. His long friendship with South Africa started in 1948, when on the first tour after the war, England visited South Africa. Since that first meeting in the fifties I have had the pleasure of meeting Denis Compton on and off for the next thirty years or so.

## TOMMY TRINDER

Streatham-born comedian Tommy Trinder was the first liner passenger ever to arrive at Southampton in a helicopter.

*Tommy Trinder – with briefcase.* Planet News

In March 1960 he was booked to make an eight week tour covering Durban, Rhodesia, Johannesburg, Port Elizabeth, and Cape Town. On the day he was due to sail in the *Stirling Castle*, he had to attend a luncheon in London to present a cheque for the London Boy's Clubs to Prince Philip, the Duke of Edinburgh. Explaining the need for speedy transport in order "to catch the boat for South Africa," Trinder was picked by Prince Philip, who said, "Boat? Don't you mean ship?"

"Well, Sir," said Trinder cheekily, "all I know is that my wife and daughter have gone down to Southampton on the Boat Train!"

As soon as the lunch was over, Trinder was taken by motor cycle to Battersea Heliport and then flown to the docks in a Westland Widgeon helicopter, the journey taking three quarters of an hour. At the helicopter landing site, off the new docks, Tommy Trinder was greeted by the Chief Docks Manager, who had arranged for a car to take him to the *Stirling Castle*, where his wife and daughter were waiting. This provided a field day for the publicity practitioners and photographers.

"Going back to London in the helicopter, Henry?" suggested many of the press. "Of course!" I said, little realising they were fixing it with Captain Alistair Gordon, the pilot. It proved a fascinating flight, of which I was later to receive a charming memento. Just as we took off, I gave a thumbs-up sign to the cheering journalists and was photographed. The photo, surrounded by the signatures of all those present and in a smart Hogarth frame, was presented to me a week or so later.

## KENNETH MORE

Kenneth More and his wife spent a holiday in Las Palmas, sailing there and back by Union-Castle, and I travelled down to Southampton with them on the boat train.

He was just as he appears on film and television. Average height, distinctive voice, and I was "old boy" within minutes. Kenneth More surprised me by relating that when they were making *Genevieve*,

**Kenneth More**
*www.kennethmore.fsnet.co.uk*

that delightful film about vintage cars, he frequently returned home quite despondent at the end of the day's shooting. He – and indeed the rest of the cast – regarded it as a run of the mill film and none ever envisaged it being the success it became.

As a bit of interest I produced a pre-War Windmill Theatre programme with frequent mention in the cast of the various sketches of one 'Ken More'. A photograph of the entire company included our hero in full evening dress. "Look at your hair," said his wife in some horror. Unlike this then 'natural' look, Mr More's hair was carefully parted and plastered down in the then fashionable Brylcreem way.

### THE DAGENHAM GIRL PIPERS

During this period I met many other PROs and publicity men. For sheer, infectious enthusiasm I shall always remember David Land. Best known as impresario of the highly successful rock opera *Jesus Christ Superstar*, back in 1957, he was press agent for pianist Stanley Black and the Dagenham Girl Pipers.

Land had arranged for six of the girls to form part of Wilkie's Circus which was to make a year's tour of South Africa and Rhodesia. He invited me to his small Wardour Street office to discuss arrangements for publicity on sailing day – which included piping the girls out of Waterloo Station on the boat train.

He carried me along with him by his absolute ardour and was the first person I

*A group of Dagenham Girl Pipers are piped out of Waterloo Station en route to Southampton to catch the Mailship for Cape Town.* Sport & General

had heard to use the phrase 'captured the public's imagination,' a statement he made on more than one occasion about the girls of whom he was obviously proud. Sailing day was a publicity riot, what with the pipes and the tears and the cheers.

Of course, passengers such as Steele, Trinder and the Girl Pipers presented me with few, if any, problems, being more than anxious to meet the press. The publicity that accrued to us was good 'fun to travel by Union-Castle' stuff.◆

## CHAPTER NINE

# THE END OF THE LINE

1959 started with the maiden voyage of the *Pendennis Castle*, followed in June by the launch of *Windsor Castle* by the Queen Mother, and ended with my being head-hunted for an important new post in South Africa's UK wine trade.

In early November 1959 a London firm of management consultants approached me and invited me to call on them at their offices. They told me that the South African Winefarmer's Association based in the City, were then enjoying increasing sales of the Cape product, especially fortified wines such as sherry and port. SAWFA, (as it was popularly known) had been asked by their parent company, the KWV (the initials of their Afrikaans name), the vast co-operative in Paarl composed of some five thousand wine farmers at the Cape, to set up a publicity department to help increase sales even further.

To this end they sought a specialist in press and public relations, advertising, sales promotion and publicity generally, together with a degree of marketing and research knowledge, and the consultants said they thought I fitted the bill. "Naturally I am flattered," I said, "but in all fairness I know very little about wine."

"But you know about publicity," they responded. They then offered me the job.

Union-Castle had long played a vital role in the UK marketing of Cape Wines as the weekly mail service to Southampton enabled SAWFA to plan a schedule of shipping requirements well in advance. Some of the best products from the historic Cape winelands were, of course, included on the Union-Castle wine lists.

In addition, both *Windsor Castle* and *Transvaal Castle* had been fitted with wine tanks. The total tankage capacity of *Windsor Castle* was 81 000 gallons, with the largest tank taking 27 000 gallons. There were in all seven tanks, which could be emptied at a rate of 12 000 gallons an hour.

The connection was strong and would mean my maintaining continued contact with the Line. I told the consultants I must think about it, which I did, long and hard, with Linda and close friends. I met those at the top of SAWFA and, finally, decided to accept the offer.

South of the equator the seasons are, of course, reversed, so, with their summer holidays, Christmas and the New Year, it was February 1960 before my new appointment was confirmed by the KWV Board at the Cape.

The Cayzers were initially shocked – indeed even angry – when I tendered my resignation, but gradually became reconciled to the fact, in due course seeking my thoughts as regards my successor. Should they go outside or appoint a replacement from within the organisation. My advice was the latter, especially as in my deputy, Sydney Smith, they had surely the ideal man. Ideal because of his tremendous application to details, which, having established as I had that it was "fun to sail with Union-Castle", was essential to underwriting the whole approach to the future.

Sydney had joined Union-Castle in 1927 and had been a long time member of the Line's publicity department, where his principal responsibilities were assistant editorship of the Gordon Brown Guide Books and administrator-cum-organiser of special functions, launch parties, and the like. He was responsible for the impeccable travel and other arrangements for the *Windsor Castle* launch party to Birkenhead. On return to Union-Castle following his war service, Sydney had set to in his spare time to study for a Bachelor of Science degree in Economics and had achieved it with honours – an effort that had my unstinting admiration.

News of my resignation had by then, however, reached Ken McArthur, my opposite number in Cape Town, who immediately applied for my job. The Cayzers were not averse to this, but wanted McArthur to stay on in Cape Town until the *Windsor Castle* had made her maiden voyage in August 1960. This did not suit McArthur who wanted to quit South Africa at once, having just separated from his wife.

The Cayzers were adamant, but so determined was Ken to leave South Africa that he resigned from Union-Castle and joined the Heller organisation on the understanding that they posted him to their London office in the City. He came and saw me. He had lost a tremendous amount of weight and looked positively scrawny. It was sad to see this hitherto dynamic character looking so sorry for himself.

Then the incredible happened. Ken McArthur applied for and got the post of publicity manager for the City of Durban. His wife, with whom he had continued to correspond, agreed to take him back. All seemed set for the fairy tale ending, but Ken had only been back a fortnight with his wife in Durban when he had a brain haemorrhage and died – all of which I found so very sad.

Things then moved quickly. In early March Sydney Smith's appointment as my replacement was confirmed and he and I were invited to luncheon with Sir Nicholas Cayzer and members of the Board. At the end of the month I hosted a farewell luncheon with my many press friends on board *Pendennis Castle* (a name seldom out of my mind the previous year) and how apt, too, that the dining saloon should carry a splendid mural of a Cape vineyard. On my final day with Union-Castle I was rewarded with a voyage to Madeira and back, with a short stay at *Reid's Hotel*, with the family.

Come June it was time for us to start packing for 'Holiday of a lifetime 2.' On 16 June 1960 there we were were again, on board the mailship at Southampton on a Thursday waiting for four o'clock. We found life on board as exciting and satisfying as ever and quickly fell into the routine again.

All too soon it was Sunday and just over forty miles from Madeira the small island of Porto Santo was passed on the starboard side. Its magnificent stretch of beach gleamed in the afternoon sun and it had all the appearance of a desert island, although we were told it was much favoured as a holiday retreat by wealthy Portuguese.

**'Farewell' Luncheon with Press.** *Union-Castle*

Soon gulls were circling the mast and about 5 pm we entered the blue waters of Funchal Bay. Most of the passengers had been crowding the ship's rails ever since Porto Santo was sighted and now we all watched fascinated as a fleet of small boats surrounded *Winchester Castle* as she reached her anchorage.

Some of the boatmen had embroidery, wickerwork, and souvenirs for sale, but the majority of the rowing boats carried young boys who would dive for coins tossed into the clear waters by the passengers. The whole scene had a degree of frenzy about it, with the little rowing boats constantly jostling each other for a better position, and their occupants keeping up a steady chorus of shouts for attention. Immediately below us a sturdy young man held, at arms length, above his head, a boy of about ten, shouting, "My brother him good boy," and then threw him into the sea, whilst from the rear of the armada came a call at regular intervals for, 'Mr. Brown.' I liked the simple philosophy of his sales technique. It assumed that in every shipload of passengers there would be a Mr Brown who, hopefully, would respond to the calling of his name. Obviously no market research could have been undertaken to confirm the assumption. The fact that his sales patter did not include the Smiths and the Jones' could only be attributed to the influence locally of Mr A Gordon Brown of Guide Book fame.

A launch soon had us ashore and a truly ancient car with the hood down conveyed us up the hill to *Reid's Hotel*, where a splendid suite of rooms overlooking the bay had been reserved for us. We only had twenty-four hours on the island before embarking on the *Pretoria Castle* for the homeward voyage, so Linda and I were determined to make the most of it.

The great attraction of breakfast out on the verandah the next morning, was the wide variety of lizards, both large and small, that would suddenly dart around our feet for crumbs or similar morsels before disappearing

in a flash. Avril did a lot of swimming and diving, whilst a charming Portuguese boy took Stephen rowing out into the bay. Lunch was one of the truly memorable occasions. Although it was out of season, the orchestra was there and playing, and there was a full complement of waiters. The restaurant had recently undergone certain renovations, including the installation of an enormous picture window overlooking Funchal Bay. What with the food, the wine, the service, the view, and the music, it was a magical event.

All too soon the tall figure of Graham Blandy, the Union-Castle agent in Funchal, was there to escort us by his private launch to *Pretoria Castle*. On board we found our good friend, Captain John Fisher, resplendent in white tropical suit, coping with an ambitious diving boy who, having collected £6 from passengers in return for which he had dived from the bridge, now wished for a further £6 to repeat the exercise, but this time finishing up once he had hit the water by swimming under the ship and coming up the other side. Captain Fisher said a very firm, "No", so the lad dived over the side, swam to one of the boats and proceeded to offer his services as a diver for coins.

We went slightly mad as regards souvenirs. In addition to a large wooden sailing ship, a wooden work basket, and an embroidered shopping basket – we bought two wickerwork garden chairs, which only recently have started to break up. These were hauled on board by rope and the money passed down the same way.

All too soon the voyage was over, we tied up at Southampton and were on our way to London on the Boat Train. We had arranged for a car to meet us at Waterloo station. Although it was a limousine of the type that has two tip-up seats in addition to a back seat taking three in comfort, the only way we could accommodate our two Madeira wicker chairs was by not using the tip-up seats and placing the chairs in the space then available. Avril and Stephen sat

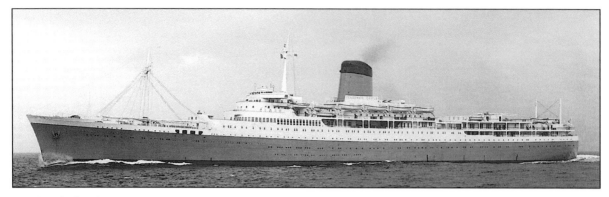

**Pendennis Castle**

in them, riding home in some state as these seats were higher than the car seats. This caused considerable curiosity and many a head turned as we drove by.

Among the post awaiting us at home was a letter from SAWFA telling me that the Board had invited me to visit the Cape winelands on a two week educational trip in mid July – only three weeks away. It proved a fascinating experience but that is another story.

I continued to keep in touch with Union-Castle and the travel trade generally, for which I know I shall always retain a particular affection.

In August 1960 *Windsor Castle* made her maiden voyage, and in January 1961, Lady Cayzer, the wife of Sir Nicholas, launched the *Transvaal Castle*. These two great new mailships, together with *Pendennis Castle*, replaced *Arundel Castle* which made her final voyage in 1921, *Carnarvon Castle* (1926) and *Winchester Castle* (1930) – three grand old ladies who owed the Line nothing.

Soon to be pensioned off were *Stirling Castle* (1930), *Athlone Castle* (1930) and *Capetown Castle* (1938), their place in the mail fleet to be taken by two new Super Cargo Liners with no passenger accommodation. They were named *Good Hope Castle* and *Southampton Castle*.

**Southampton Castle**

The year 1962 saw the end of Union-Castle's 'Round Africa' service, which had served South and especially East Africa so well for forty years. The 'Winds of change' so accurately forecast by Prime Minister Harold Macmillan in 1960 had already begun in the Belgian Congo. One by one each Colony sought and obtained self-government.

Inevitably, this resulted in the number of officials and administrators from Britain and Europe decreasing. Those that remained had to agree to new terms of service, which included shorter home leave, which they were encouraged to take by air. Those travelling for pleasure were increasingly tempted by package tours involving travel by air.

Consequently the three new one-class ships bravely built by Sir Vernon Thomson in the early fifties reached the end of their service little over ten years later. First to be sold was the *Rhodesia Castle* which arrived at Kaosiung in October 1967 for demolition, followed by the *Braemar Castle*. Luckier was their sister ship, *Kenya Castle*, for she was sold to the Chandris group, who renamed her *Amerikanis* (American lady) and cruised her from America to the West Indies.

In July 1965 the new faster mail service was introduced, with the first sailing being taken taken by the flagship *Windsor Castle*. The voyage time was reduced from fourteen to eleven and a half days, which meant the new schedule could be operated by seven liners instead of eight. It also necessitated ending every Thursday at 4 o'clock as the mailship did not have to leave Southampton until 1 pm on Fridays. Not unnaturally, I felt sad at this break with a longstanding tradition, but at least the famous Union-Castle mail service to the Cape was still operating.

Towards the end of 1965 another announcement was made which caused considerable interest, particularly in South Africa. Union-Castle concluded an agreement with the South African Marine Corporation, giving the latter a participation in the mail service. *Transvaal Castle* and *Pretoria Castle* were sold to Safmarine who renamed them *SA Vaal* and *SA Oranje*. Although they then sailed in Safmarine colours they continued to be managed by Union-Castle.

By the end of 1973 oil prices had rocketed and shipping companies had to look to ways of cutting back on the amount of fuel used – and of increasing their revenue. Union-Castle decided that the mailship would slow down by taking an extra day on the voyage to and from South Africa – and increase fares.

Then, in freight shipping circles, the talk was all of containerisation. Quicker than that British & Commonwealth Shipping Company joined with others such as Furness Withy to form O.C.L. – Overseas Containers Limited.

What is containerisation? Whereas, in the past, freight was passed down to the relevant docks by road and rail, for loading on board and stowing in the ship's holds, containerisation is a far simpler exercise – and therefore economic in every sense. Items to be shipped are initially packed into a container. Two standard sizes of container are employed – twenty foot and forty foot. These are easily conveyed down to the docks on rail or road transporters specially designed to accommodate them. The containers are then packed on special container ships, and this operation becomes almost child's play as it's like a child building with bricks.

The Union-Castle mailships, although designed to carry both passengers and cargo, were not suitable for the conveyance of containers, which even sit on deck in solid ranks. Unattractive they may be to the eye, but most attractive as regards the accounts in that the inevitable saving, both in time and manpower, can in no way be ignored. Pilferage is also considerably reduced. As one person put it, "No great style, but, by golly isn't it efficient?" Once a container fleet had been built up, the traditional ships were doomed.

AROUND THIS TIME the Union-Castle publicity department produced a unique poster headlined 'The Big Five to South Africa'. It depicted the five passenger mailships steaming from left to right in line abreast and was a masterpiece of the photographer's art, proving yet again that the camera can most certainly lie.

In June 1974 *Windsor Castle* completed her one-hundredth voyage between Southampton and Cape Town. She had by then sailed 1.4 million miles without missing one scheduled sailing.

But a month earlier the weekly news magazine *To the Point* had reported: "The era of the giant liners, often termed by the leisurely-minded as 'floating hotels', is on the verge of becoming no more than a nostalgic memory."

Six months later, *Travel Trade Gazette* carried the banner headline "Union-Castle fights to keep its passenger service". The story beneath read: "Union-Castle's chief passenger

Indeed, so successful was the lie that one purserette was heard to wonder how it had been possible to bring all these great ships together at one and the same time and wasn't it dangerous to have them sailing so close together?

manager, Mr John Andreae, is hopeful that passenger services to South Africa will continue into the 1980s despite plans to containerise the route. "With five ships left on the route operating about thirty-six round trips a year, it's the last liner operation of any size left in the world," he said."

Towards the end of that year I had lunch with an old friend from my Union-Castle days and asked about the future of the passenger fleet. He painted a very gloomy picture. Of the five mailships he pointed out that the *SA Oranje* (the former *Pretoria Castle*) had recently made her last

**The 33 697grt. mailship SA Vaal sails from Cape Town for the last time.** *Safmarine*

voyage, whilst the *Edinburgh Castle* would be withdrawn from service in the spring of 1976.

The *SA Vaal* (formerly *Transvaal Castle*) would be retained by Safmarine for prestige purposes, whilst, "The *Pendennis Castle*, he said, "will be axed sooner than you might think – possibly next year."

"Will Union-Castle retain the *Windsor Castle* for prestige purposes?" I asked.

"The passenger service is losing millions of pounds a year," he replied. "All the passenger ships will have gone within the next two years."

I felt particularly sad about the *Pendennis Castle*, for which, not unnaturally, I claim some sort of special relationship, and took the opportunity of a chance meeting with James Thomson, the group's financial director, to quiz him about the future. His answer was succinct, to the point, and, sadly irrefutable. "When, in one year, a ship shows a loss of a million pounds I am prepared to ignore it," he said, "but when that ship goes on year after year making such a loss, I cannot ignore it."

The writing was well and truly on the wall, and on 8 January 1976, the respected shipping journal, *Lloyds List*, under the headline 'Two more liners to be withdrawn from South African service', wrote:

Two passenger cargo liners operating on the Union-Castle Line service to South Africa are to be withdrawn this year, the *Edinburgh Castle* in April and *Pendennis Castle* in June, leaving only two liners, *Windsor Castle* and *SA Vaal*, on a route which once employed eight liners with one held in reserve in Southampton in case of breakdown. It is not surprising that the *Edinburgh Castle* is coming out of service as she is now twenty-seven years old, being one of the first mailships planned as the last war was ending. Always a good sea boat she has been extremely popular, attracting her own quota of passengers.

The *Pendennis Castle*, however is a much younger ship. Completed at Harland & Wolff's Belfast shipyard late in 1958, she sailed on her maiden voyage from Southampton to the Cape on New Year's Day, 1959. It was a great occasion, for the *Pendennis Castle* was the first ship to enter service after the Union-Castle/Clan Line merger, and on sailing day it was announced that the ship's master, the late Captain George Mayhew, had been made a CBE, so today the Liner is only seventeen years old."

"On Monday 14 June 1976, flying a paying off pennant from her mainmast, the *Pendennis Castle* docked at Southampton after her last voyage from South Africa." That is how the *Southern Evening Echo's* shipping column reporter, Arthur Taylor, started his story of the withdrawal from the Cape route of this victim of soaring costs. In a letter to me at the time Arthur wrote:

> The last arrival was a sad occasion. When an old liner like the *Edinburgh Castle* was withdrawn, it did not seem too much out of place, but withdrawal of a seventeen year old vessel like the *Pendennis Castle* seems to be a disaster, especially as a question mark hangs over the future of the Windsor and the Vaal.

*Pendennis Castle* was sold and sailed to Hong Kong where she was renamed *Ocean Queen* and seemed destined for cruising. The following year she was given a couple of new names – *Sinbad*, then *Sinbad I* – but never traded. She headed for Taiwan in 1980, and was later broken up.

In early 1977 it was announced that both *Windsor Castle* and *SA Vaal* would be withdrawn from service later that year. In April that year I escorted a large party of Masters of Wine to the Cape winelands and on the return flight discovered the current copy of *The Flying Springbok*, South African Airways' in-flight magazine, carried on its cover a magnificent photograph of *Windsor Castle* sailing from Cape Town, with the decks lined with passengers throwing streamers. The leading article inside – 'The Passing of the Mail Fleet' – ran to three superbly illustrated pages. The piece, written by Judith Berrisford, with great affection, ended:

> Magnificent the mailships may have been, luxurious, superlative – but for one thing above all others they will be remembered: they were the friendliest among ships.
> "Well", said someone, cynically, "They can afford to be generous now that the competition of Union-Castle is to be no more." Maybe, but I prefer to think that this was a gesture recognising the part the Line had played in the progress of South Africa.

**Ship by night.**

*Windsor Castle's* final voyage was scheduled for Friday 12 August 1977. A special luncheon, arranged and hosted by Sir Nicholas Cayzer was held on board on Wednesday 10 August 1977. To our delight Linda and I were invited – despite the fact that I had left the company nearly twenty years earlier. It was both a sad day and a memorable one, but certainly an occasion we felt very privileged to attend. In his speech welcoming the guests, Sir Nicholas said he saw this as the end of an era more relaxed and enjoyable than today and a more gracious age to live in.

Departure, two days later, was delayed for an hour owing to a signal failure causing the late arrival at Southampton Docks of the Boat Train from Waterloo station. *Windsor Castle* eventually sailed on her last voyage to Cape Town at 2pm carrying some 800 passengers, cargo, and, of course, mail. Despite the delay, this final sailing for Union-Castle was attended with great ceremony, including a RAF flypast – quite a distinction that. The next day the *Southern Evening Echo* carried a picture of *Windsor Castle* sailing down the Solent with, below, a photograph from California of the Space Shuttle orbiter off for its first free flight. It was captioned – 'Age makes way.'

At precisely 4 pm on Tuesday 6 September, the Line's flagship left Cape Town amidst tears and cheers, the singing of *Auld Lang Syne* and a water cannon salute from two tugs. She was escorted out of Table Bay by a South African Naval frigate which fired a shot across the bows of *Windsor Castle* and ordered her to heave to. From the frigate a party of 'pirates' boarded the liner and captured the bridge where they presented Captain Beadon with an embroidered mailbag.

In mid September *Windsor Castle* completed her final round voyage. This is how *Daily Express* feature writer John Rydon described the scene: "She crept up the Solent in the dawn light trailing a wistful pennant of dark smoke. Attendant tugs nudged her lilac hull into Southampton's 102 berth. *Windsor Castle*, flagship of the once mighty Union-Castle Line, was coming home from the South African run for the last time."

Being her last voyage, many went ashore with souvenirs. Chief Purser John Dinimock reported a clock lost in Durban, and a plaque in Port Elizabeth. He added, "And see there's a picture missing on the stairs."

Ever since her maiden voyage seventeen years earlier, Dusty Miller had been the First Class dining room manager. He enthused about the send-off they were given in Cape Town. "Two military bands and a flypast – and you could hardly see the ship for streamers," he said.

**Windsor Castle** *leaving Cape Town for the last time.*

**Leaving Cape Town.**

The Greek billionaire ship owner John S. Latsis bought *Windsor Castle*, renaming her *Margarita* as a charming gesture to one of his two daughters. She left Southampton for the last time on 3 October for Piraeus, with a Greek crew and flying the Greek flag. Her famous black and red funnel was painted a deep yellow with black topping and her hull white – the colours of the new owner. On the first night at sea a Greek crewman switched off an oil pump and seized up one of the turbines. Union-Castle engineers, whose aid was called for, had to work day and night fitting new bearings to get her under way again.

She was for many years anchored in Saudi Arabia at Jeddah, the port city for Mecca, as a Panamanian-registered luxury hotel ship, but is now laid up at Eleusis where it is said she is in 'sound mechanical condition and has been well maintained.'

John Latsis died in Athens, aged nine-ty-two, in April 2003 and *Windsor Castle* could well be sold for scrap, but an attempt is being made to save her from the breakers by the setting up of the 'Mailship Windsor Castle Project.'

The *RMS Windsor Castle Preservation Society* was launched, appropriately, in Southampton and aims to raise the necessary funds to bring the ship back to Britain to be berthed at a UK port as a hotel-cum-museum. While a most attractive idea, the finance that would be involved is somewhat daunting. To buy her would cost at least £2 million, while towing her back to the UK a further £1-2 million. It is estimated that restoration to her original condition would come to around £20-40 million, and then there is maintenance, insurance, security, and so on. Nevertheless, one wished the society every success, but it was not to be for the Latsis family have now sold the ship for scrap.

*RMS* **Windsor Castle** *sails down the Solent from Southampton Docks on her last voyage to Cape Town in August 1977.*

*Windsor Castle* is one of only three laid up ocean liners in the world that survive in near original condition. The other two are *MS Augustus* and *SS Rotterdam*, and in July 2003 came news that the latter had been saved. The Holland-America Line's former flagship was sold to her original builders, the Rotterdam Drydock Company, who plan to berth her – after a two year refurbishment in Rotterdam.

But there was no such luck for *Transvaal Castle*, the last passenger mailship ordered by Union-Castle. At the time of the announcement that *SS Rotterdam* had been successfully preserved came a report that the former mailship had been sold to Indian breakers. Sold to Safmarine and renamed *SA*

*Vaal*, she ended the historic 120-year-old mail service to the Cape in October 1977. She then sailed to Japan for refitting prior to being sold to Carnival Cruise Lines, Florida. Again, renamed *Festivale*, her new owners described her as 37 175 tonnes of fun. Twenty years later, now as *Island Breeze*, she joined Premier Cruises' fleet, but remained inactive for two years, when she received her fifth name as *Big Red Boat IV* – and was laid up in the Bahamas. It was hoped she would be able to sail to India under her own steam in 2003, despite engine failure and a power blackout.

*Southampton Castle* made the last ever mailship voyage from the UK to South Africa, returning to Southampton on 2 October 1977.

So ended a long tradition of service carrying mail, passengers and cargo on the Golden Run, but cargo and mail was catered for on the new container ship service in which Union-Castle, through Overseas Containers Ltd and Safmarine were taking part. Union-Castle was also managing the OCL container ship Table Bay.

A remarkable piece of maritime history, covering a period of over one hundred years and representing one of the great ocean-going passenger liner services in the world, was at an end.◆

**Festivale** *Carnival Cruise Lines*

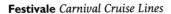

## CHAPTER TEN

# POST UNION-CASTLE/SAFMARINE 1978 – 1989

*RMS* **St. Helena**

## 1978

The little island of St Helena way out in the South Atlantic must take credit for the initial re-establishment of a route by sea to and from the Cape. Best known as Napoleon's place of exile, the British colony's only link with the world – communication systems apart – was by sea. Union-Castle provided the only regular service for the 6 500 islanders.

There was a gap for a while, but in the year the service ended, Curnow Shipping Ltd of Porthleven in Cornwall negotiated with the Government of St Helena to form the St Helena Shipping Co Ltd and place in service a ship capable of carrying both cargo and passengers to the island.

The search for such a vessel was worldwide, but eventually in Canada, they found the fifteen year old 3 150 grt *Northland Prince* which had modern accommodation for around 75 passengers. She was built on a cargo carrying hull and was an ideal choice. The vessel was renamed *St Helena*, the cere-

mony being carried out by the late Princess Margaret – the same Royal who had christened the 28 700 grt *Edinburgh Castle* in October 1947.

Less than a year after the demise of the 'Golden Run', it was again possible to sail the historic route. The new service, operated from Avonmouth to Cape Town by way of the Canaries, Ascension and St Helena, with occasional calls at St Vincent in the Cape Verde Islands, is still operating today.

In 1978 the 22 000 grt Greek liner *Navarino* (the former trans-Atlantic ship *Gripsholm*) set out from Southampton on a four and a half month winter's cruise. It started with a sixteen day voyage to Cape Town via La Palmas, thence to South America for Christmas and the New Year, eventually returning to Cape Town for return, at the end of March, to Southampton. Painted white overall, she was an attractive old-style ship with large funnels and was to make similar cruises over the next three years.

*MV WORLD RENAISSANCE*

Built in France in 1966 for trade between Marseilles and Haifa and cruising as *Renaissance* she was owned by the Greek shipping lines Epirotiki, and chartered by Costa Line in 1977. Subsequently, as *World Renaissance*, she was cruising in the Caribbean.

Each of her 220 cabins – accommodating a total of 516 passengers – was fully air conditioned with private shower/bath and toilet. With a length of 150 metres and beam of 21 metres, *World Renaissance* was equipped with stabilisers and capable of speeds of up to 18 knots.

In mid-2003 an advertisement in the travel section of one of the Sunday newspapers caught my eye. It was for 'cruise holidays' in the lands of the Bible, for which the operator, MasterSun, used two vessels – *Ocean Majesty* and *World Renaissance*.

I sent for details and the picture of the vessel showed her looking much the same, except that her original white hull was now painted black and her former yellow funnel appeared to be blue. A comparison of the two deck plans showed little change except that the various decks had all been given Greek god and goddess names, for example, the former restaurant deck was now *Dionysus Deck* and the Grand Salon Deck, *Apollo Deck*.

Still going strong at the ripe old age of thirty-seven – despite her troubles in 1984!

## 1979

Two years after the cessation of the mail service, the Italian Lauro Line proudly announced that once again a liner would sail between the United Kingdom and South Africa – and that they were placing their flagship, the 23 862 grt *Achille Lauro*, the pride of their fleet – 'a beautiful ship, designed in the grand style of the great Atlantic liners' – on the route.

She left Southampton at the end of November 1979 for a fourteen-day voyage to the Cape and, after cruising in the Indian Ocean, she departed on the northbound trip in Mid-January 1980. She was to repeat the round voyage the following year.

## 1982

Curnow Shipping continued to operate their service to the Cape via the two islands, but with the outbreak of war in the Falklands, their splendid little ship was requisitioned by the Ministry of Defence in May 1982, for 'support operations.' She joined the task force, firstly as a mine-sweeper support vessel, and then as a passenger-supply ship between Ascension Island and the Falklands.

Curnow Shipping were fortunate, however, to have under their management from Silvermist Properties the 698 grt twelve-passenger *Aragonite*, which was immediately chartered by St Helena Shipping to enable their Cape service to continue. Known affectionately by the St Helenians as "the twelve-seater bus", *Aragonite* covered some 77 000 miles during her time with St Helena Shipping from 1982 to October 1983.

## 1983

In August 1983 came exciting news. The St Helena Shipping Co announced that, in conjunction with one of South Africa's leading tour operators, TFC, they were chartering the 8 665 grt cruise liner *World Renaissance* 'to revive', as they proudly put it, 'a regular luxury liner service to Cape Town, in the tradition of the great ocean liners.'

That October Allan Foggitt, a TFC director, over from South Africa, called on me at the Cape Wine Centre (which I had set up in 1978) to discuss the famous run and to introduce the managing director of their UK operation, Perl Lederer. Later that month Linda and I were invited to 'a promotion of the luxury liner service *World Renaissance* to South Africa' at the *Selfridge Hotel* in London's Oxford Street. We found Perl and her TFC colleagues in an upbeat mood. She told me, "We're here to celebrate successful sales of the new service."

On a table at the back of the room was a large model of *World Renaissance* – in ice. The guest list was headed by the South African ambassador, the Hon. Marius Steyn and his wife (he spoke with affection of sailing in the *Capetown Castle* some years back). Also there were Jock Webster, Satour's PRO, John Lancaster-Smith of the Passenger Shipping Association who, in a brief address to the guests, described the ship as 'comfortable and friendly' and former Union-Castle man John Knighton, then with Musgrove and Watson at their West End office. It was a happy occasion, full of enthusiasm for the new venture.

Informal discussions continued with TFC and prior to *World Renaissance's* inaugural voyage to the Cape due to leave Plymouth on 25 November, Perl asked if I would be prepared to give a talk and tasting

of Cape wines during the second voyage leaving the UK on Saturday, 28 January, 1984. In addition, would I submit a confidential report on the voyage? "I shall need to have the woman's point of view," I said. "Of course, Linda must go with you," responded Perl.

The *World Renaissance's* charter was due to expire in early 1984, when the plan was to lease from the German company HADAG, the 18 834 grt West German cruise ship *Astor*. Sadly, all these plans were doomed to failure.

At that time there was considerable speculation that Safmarine was to re-enter the passenger ship service to and from South Africa. Only twelve days before the TFC inaugural voyage to the Cape, the rumour was proved right. Large advertisements appeared in the national press headlined: 'In April 1984 you can begin to re-live fond memories in style.' Ironically, Safmarine was to operate their new service with the *Astor*, which they had by then purchased.

Four weeks later, just a week before *World Renaissance* was due to sail from Plymouth, Curnow Shipping decided reluctantly to pull out, saying it had little chance of surviving a fares battle 'with a group as powerful as Safmarine.' TFC had little option but to carry on alone, but their troubles were far from over.

*World Renaissance* departed in late November in pouring rain with rumours of gales ahead, which duly materialised, finishing with a severe storm in the Bay of Biscay. It was not until the vessel was south of Portugal some days later that the weather improved. By now the ship was well behind schedule, so that when she reached Las Palmas a day late, the three hundred passengers were only allowed ashore for two and a half hours.

After this, life on board did settle down into a more peaceful routine – that is, until arrival at Freetown in Sierra Leone. Here, more precious time was lost by the inefficiency of the local dock labourers, not only in securing the vessel alongside, but also in

## Cruise liner turns back to Spain after captain refuses to cross bay

# Crew's fear over Biscay Triangle

*WORLD RENAISSANCE : Lisbon last stop.*

**by Keith Dovkants**

A BRITISH shipping company today flew passengers to their cruise liner in Lisbon because the captain would not cross the Biscay Triangle.

The so-called Triangle between Land's End and Spain had earlier claimed two other ships, one of which disappeared mysteriously only two weeks ago.

Captain Simon Sugrue, a director of the Cornish line Curnow Shipping which uses the World Renaissance on charter for a regular service between Plymouth and Capetown, said: "They simply refused to sail.

World Renaissance put into Lisbon after encountering bad conditions on the edge of the Biscay area.

A spokesman for TFC Tours, who sell cruises aboard the ship, said: "We were told that the captain was not prepared to risk the ship in those conditions."

The World Renaissance is Greek-owned and operated by Costa, who use Italian officers and a crew of several nationalities.

When they refused to sail last Saturday Curnow flew 150 passengers to Lisbon where the ship was berthed.

Then 100 passengers who had expected to sail across Biscay to Plymouth were flown home to Britain.

The ship is due to return from South Africa, again across Biscay, to Plymouth at the end of February.

A spokesman for Costa, the operators in London, said: "The decision to put back into Lisbon was made from concern for the safety and comfort of passengers.

"This is of paramount importance for us and in the circumstances the passengers suffered the minimum of inconvenience."

The Tito Campanella is officially "overdue" after sending an "all's well" message two weeks ago 350 miles off Land's End.

Nothing has been heard of her since and the fate of the 22,000-ton vessel and that of another Italian ship, the Marina di Equa, has produced an extraordinary reaction.

The two missing ships were cited by crewmen working for an Italian company when they refused to take the World Renaissance across the bay last weekend.

A giant whirlpool effect could be behind disappearances in the Biscay Triangle, author and naval historian John Harris said today.

Mr Harris, who has made a study of sea mysteries for his book Without Trace, said from his home in Sussex: "The idea of ships disappearing up to Mars from the Biscay or any other triangle is silly.

"But the fact remains that they do disappear and when there are no survivors you have a mystery.

### Hove-to

"The Bay of Biscay has always had this notoriety and I remember being hove-to there in a convoy during the war for days. We dare not move because of the fierce conditions. We were just hanging on.

"It could be that as these storms come through and the rollers sweep across the Atlantic from the west they are deflected somehow by the curve of the coast, creating a sort of whirlpool.

"Seamen have feared the place for centuries and when you have the fact of a ship simply vanishing it's easy to see why."

The Tito Campanella was carrying a cargo of sheet metal, a notoriously difficult material to secure in extreme conditions.

Shifting cargo is responsible for many sinkings but if this did occur it still doesn't explain why the ship sent out no SOS.

The vessel was fully equipped with long-range and VHF radios, including back-up sets.

A search of the area in which it disappeared by planes and other vessels, has so far revealed no trace of wreckage.

---

refilling the fresh water tanks. In order to catch the tide the ship had to leave before the refilling had been completed – with the result that water on board had to be rationed.

The call at St Helena was to have been one of the highlights of the voyage. However, still twelve hours behind schedule, it was getting dark when anchored off Jamestown at 7 pm and she was off again at midnight. Despite all these disasters the ship did in fact arrive at Cape Town on schedule at 7.30 am on Monday 12 December, 1983.

So severe had been the storm in the Bay of Biscay that on the return leg – with similar weather forecast – the captain halted the voyage at Lisbon 'in the interests of the safety and comfort of passengers.' In fact, the crew had refused to cross the Biscay Triangle. The so-called Triangle between Land's End and Spain had earlier claimed two other ships, one of which had disappeared mysteriously only two weeks earlier.

The result was that Linda and I, together with the other one hundred and fifty or so passengers booked on the second

voyage to Cape Town, had to be flown out to Portugal, while those who were northbound were brought to the UK by air, or, in some cases, overland – all at considerable cost to the operator.

# Liner's crew's fear of Biscay ended voyage

**By JOHN PETTY Shipping Correspondent**

PASSENGERS have been airlifted from Britain to Portugal because the crew of a liner feared crossing the stormy Bay of Biscay and ended the voyage at Lisbon.

"We are dismayed by their attitude," said Cornish-based Curnow Shipping, which has the 12,000-ton Italian - operated, Greek - owned World Renaissance on charter for a regular service between Plymouth and Cape Town.

Costa, the company which operates the 220-cabin six-deck liner, notified Curnow that the voyage had been halted in the interests of the "safety and comfort" of the passengers.

But it appears that many of the crew were unwilling to go through the severe storms ahead. The officers are Italian and the crew multi-national.

About 150 passengers had to be flown out to Lisbon and a further 100, who had been northbound, brought back.

Now Costa is putting in at an extra port, Madeira, as compensation to passengers.

The service began in November as the first regular passenger line to Cape Town since Union Castle quit the route in 1977.

## 1984

Our trip started at London Gatwick Airport, from where, on Saturday, 28 January, 1984, we flew off by TAP Air Portugal to reach Lisbon in time for a 10.30 pm *bon voyage* dinner on board. The next day we assembled at 9 am for a tour of Lisbon prior to sailing for Madeira, an additional port of call offered as compensation for the inconvenience we had all been caused. We left promptly at four o'clock – nice touch that, albeit that it was Sunday.

John Lancaster-Smith's description of *World Renaissance* as 'comfortable and friendly' was epitomised by the ship's master Captain Yiannis Papadopoulos. Tall, slim and a bearded Gregory Peck look-alike, he was quite happy for passengers to visit him at any time on that holy-of-holies, the Bridge. The Wheelhouse had Donald Duck painted in full colour on one side and Pluto on the other.

Captain Papadopoulos was Greek, as were his officers. Stewards for cabins and in the dining saloon were mainly Spanish-speaking, but we all got by. For example, our cabin stewardess, Melin, was from Honduras, as was our restaurant steward, Miguel, and Armelfo was from Guatemala. Our wine waiter was Jane, an ex-Butlin's girl from Wigan.

Many of the passengers were former Union-Castle regulars and it was obvious that the opportunity to again sail the 'Golden Run' had been most welcome. All the usual deck games were available. At eleven o'clock sharp

*Captain Papadopoulos welcomes Linda aboard* **World Renaissance.**

cups of bouillon, the traditional beef tea, were served, making one feel one was an invalid recovering from a serious illness, but in fact intended to keep one going from a large breakfast to an equally large lunch. Soon, we all started throwing pre-lunch champagne parties out on deck prior to lunch – in short a very good time was had by all.

After Madeira, we called at Las Palmas and then Freetown in Sierra Leone before the long haul to St Helena prior to docking at Cape Town. So dire had been the warnings given us by John Sullivan regarding muggings in Freetown that Linda and I, and others, decided to remain on board and sunbathe.

The highlight of the ports of calls was undoubtedly that at St Helena, unfortunately missed out by those on the inaugural voyage.

**World Renaissance**

The good people living on the little island made us most welcome and drove us around in their own cars. The attractions were many – the Governor's residence, where a tortoise said to be two hundred years old lives in the grounds; Lansdowne House, Napoleon's exile residence (there were two gendarmes at the gates – what a posting); and the 699 steps up Jacob's Ladder, to look down on the anchorage at James Bay far below. Only one accepted the challenge to climb up all the way – our cruise director John Sullivan.

Several of the more elderly passengers were not particularly happy with some of the cruise-style entertainment. The Union-Castle voyage was not a cruise, but a line voyage, hence liner and not cruise ship. This was summed up by a conversation I overheard between a youngish passenger and an older one. "Oh dear," said the young one, "we dock tomorrow at Cape Town." "Thank goodness!" said the older one. But like the majority of those on board, we agreed with Satour's Jock Webster, who was on the inaugural voyage: "Bliss – sheer bliss," was his verdict. Linda and I spent a few days in the Cape visiting colleagues and friends before flying home.

*World Renaissance* duly returned to the UK with her charter expired and, once more part of the Epirotiki fleet, she commenced cruising in the calm waters of the Aegean and Eastern Mediterranean Sea. I was due to retire at the end of 1984, having stayed on at the request of KWV until aged sixty-six, so that the *World Renaissance* trip was a good start to this important year in my career.

Publicity for SAF Marine's *Astor* service on the 'Golden Run' was now well under way. That first fourteen and a half by ten and three quarter inch advertisement in the *Sunday Express* dated 13 November 1983, stated that, "Advance rumours of our plans have leaked out, resulting in a flood of inquiries. We are therefore opening reservations with immediate effect, well in advance of our envisaged date."

Overall marketing for the venture was in the hands of passenger manager, Len Wilton. He had resigned from P&O ("At some financial loss," he told me) to undertake the appointment which he carried out with tireless energy and great enthusiasm. The publicity material, for example, was superb and consisted mainly of two magnif-

**MS Astor**

**MS ASTOR – FACT FILE**
    Tonnage: 19 000 grt
    Length: 164 m
    Width: 22,6 m
    Built: 1981
    Ship's registry: Cape Town, South Africa
    Number of decks: 10
    Number of suites: 36
    Number of cabins: 224

Capacity: maximum 580 passengers
Crew: 220
Elevators: 3
Pools: 2 – one indoor, one outdoor
Stabilisers: 2 AEG-Denny Brown –
    each fin 7 m
Maximum speed: 20 knots
Cruising speed: 18 knots

icent brochures, each eleven and a half inch by eight and a quarter inches. One, entitled 'Escape into another world' carried details of *Astor's* programme, while the other 'Wish you were here' was a guide to the ports of call and shore excursions. Both were copiously illustrated.

Len Wilton soon sought me out and I joined him for lunch at the Marine Club in the city: "How about you organising a tour of the Cape Winelands in connection with Astor's voyage next November – and getting a degree of sponsorship?" Since I would be escorting the tour, I thought this a brilliant idea.

Sponsorship for the tour was by *Harpers Wine & Spirit*, the leading wine trade journal and Decanter magazine, the monthly for wine consumers. The party was headed up by David Burroughs, chief executive of the Wine & Spirit Education Trust, and included a group of eight from Europe.

On Tuesday 3 April, a luncheon was held on board *Astor* to celebrate the inaugural voyage from Southampton the next day, when at 1 pm, she duly sailed out for the Cape. There she was given a great welcome, her arrival no doubt nostalgically recalling the great days of the mailships.

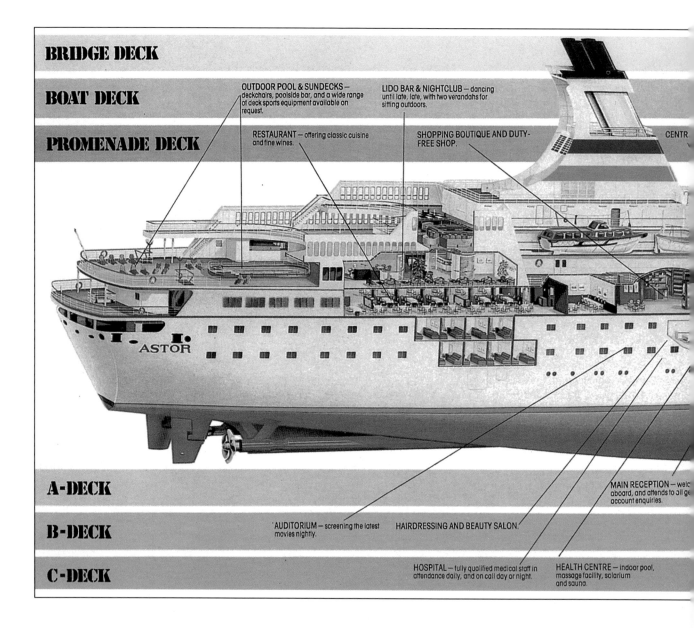

BRIDGE DECK

BOAT DECK

OUTDOOR POOL & SUNDECKS — deckchairs, poolside bar, and a wide range of deck sports equipment available on request.

LIDO BAR & NIGHTCLUB — dancing until late, late, with two verandahs for sitting outdoors.

PROMENADE DECK

RESTAURANT — offering classic cuisine and fine wines.

SHOPPING BOUTIQUE AND DUTY-FREE SHOP.

CENTR.

ASTOR

A-DECK

MAIN RECEPTION — welc aboard, and attends to all ge account enquiries.

B-DECK

AUDITORIUM — screening the latest movies nightly.

HAIRDRESSING AND BEAUTY SALON.

C-DECK

HOSPITAL — fully qualified medical staff in attendance daily, and on call day or night.

HEALTH CENTRE — indoor pool, massage facility, solarium and sauna.

She had made four round voyages and a cruise from Durban to Mauritius and the Seychelles by the autumn of 1984 when returning from Cape Town to Southampton on 6 November, history repeated itself. Once again 'gigantic waves' in the stormy Bay of Biscay, coupled with engine trouble, took their toll, resulting in *Astor* docking northbound in Lisbon, passengers again being flown back to the UK.

Instead of reviving old memories by sailing out of Southampton, we were once more flying to Portugal to join our vessel. Inconvenient maybe, but certainly a pity, as Linda and I had been invited to join Len Wilton as his guests at the annual dinner of the Passenger Shipping Association which he had cleverly arranged to be held on board Astor at Southampton the day before the scheduled departure on Thursday 22 November.

The Portuguese National Airlines specially chartered Tristar left Gatwick at noon on the 22nd to touch down at Lisbon at 2 pm, from where we were taken to the ship and settled in our cabins. We had been allocated a most comfortable suite on the port side and found to our pleasure that, the starboard side occupied by John Lancaster-Smith (Passenger Shipping Association) and his partner, Mishca.

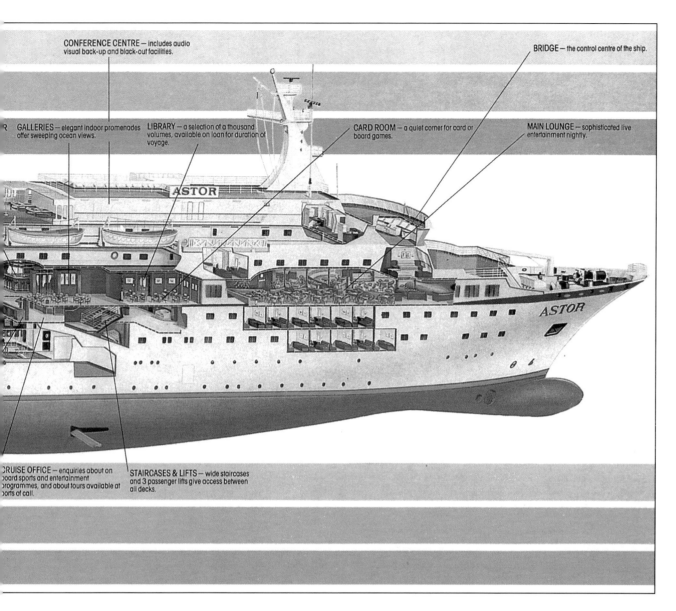

CONFERENCE CENTRE — includes audio visual back-up and black-out facilities.

BRIDGE — the control centre of the ship.

GALLERIES — elegant indoor promenades offer sweeping ocean views.

LIBRARY — a selection of a thousand volumes, available on loan for duration of voyage.

CARD ROOM — a quiet corner for card or board games.

MAIN LOUNGE — sophisticated live entertainment nightly.

CRUISE OFFICE — enquiries about on board sports and entertainment programmes, and about tours available at ports of call.

STAIRCASES & LIFTS — wide staircases and 3 passenger lifts give access between all decks.

*Disembarking at Cape Town.*

*Astor Captain's Cocktail Party: Linda with (on left) South African-born Major Norman Kark, London-based publisher of the upmarket magazine Courier, and Johannesburg journalist and short story writer Natas ('Backwards it spells Satan!' he said).*

That evening Safleisure, a division of Safmarine operating the new service, offered us all a complimentary evening excursion into Lisbon for a four course dinner in a typical restaurant with the opportunity of hearing *fados*, the nostalgic Lisbon songs, and watching some folkdancing – a great send-off for what was to prove a memorable voyage.

We sailed out of Lisbon at 8 am on Friday 23 November, and from then on it was the traditional 'Golden Run', with only one port of call, Las Palmas, before arrival fifteen nights later at Cape Town. The voyage was a delight with charming fellow passengers, many of them having sailed Union-Castle, and to be at sea again was sheer joy.

Talks and films on the history of the Cape wines, together with tastings of some of the many fine wines from South Africa on the *Astor* winelist, were given to the winelands party in the ship's conference room, which also provided the venue for the traditional cocktail party for some of our friends on board.

I was also given the opportunity of introducing the wine films on *Astor Perspective*, the ship's internal TV programme. This daily programme at 5 pm was presented by Karien van der Merwe who was a great help to me when presenting the various tastings to the group. And for good measure, I celebrated my sixty-sixth birthday during the voyage.

In short, a glorious fifteen days were spent on board *Astor* fully justifying the description of luxury liner. At Cape Town, the party checked in at the *Mount Nelson Hotel*, the ideal base from which to make daily forays into the Winelands. At the end of the tour we saw the group safely off at Cape Town airport and returned to the 'Nellie' for a few days before leaving for Johannesburg and Sabi Sabi game park. After a relaxing, but all too short stay at that magical place, Cybele Forest Lodge, it was off to Sabi Sabi for three exciting days in the Bushveld before returning home in time for Christmas celebrations with the family. So ended my full-time working career – what a way to go!

*MOUNT NELSON HOTEL*

No story of the Union-Castle Line would be complete without mention of the *Mount Nelson Hotel,* Cape Town.

Had the British Admiralty in 1857 decided not to set up a regular mail service to South Africa, the Mount Nelson Hotel might never have been built. The bid for the contract put in by the Union Line was accepted and on 15 September the 530-tonne *Dane* sailed for the Cape.

For fifteen years the Union Line had the route to themselves, but then Donald Currie, one of shipping's giants in the mid-nineteenth century, founded the Castle Line and started operating the Cape run in opposition. The challenge was on to provide ever faster sailings to South Africa.

The Union Line must have felt they had scored a considerable point when they built the *Grand Hotel* in Cape Town, but Currie was quick to retaliate with the building in 1899 of the *Mount Nelson Hotel.*

A year later the two companies merged to form the Union-Castle Mail Steamship Company Limited with Sir Donald Currie as chairman. The *Grand Hotel* remained until 1972 when it was demolished.

The "Nellie" as it is affectionately known, was designed and constructed to the highest British and European standards and still, to this day, has retained its reputation as one of the finest hotels in the world.

Winston Churchill sailed to the Cape at the turn of the century as Boer War correspondent for the *London Morning Post.* In Cape Town he stayed at the *Mount Nelson Hotel,* which had recently been built by Union-Castle to accommodate passengers sailing south to avoid the English winter "in the same style on land as they had enjoyed aboard ship." For Churchill it was 'a most excellent and well-appointed establishment.' Post-war, Sir Winston also stayed at *Reid's Palace Hotel* in Madeira.

Field-Marshall Lord Kitchener, on the other hand, was using the hotel as his headquarters, but thought it far too cushy a billet for his officers, who were duly dispatched to a tented camp in Stellenbosch. Among the hotel's other early

*Windsor Table: this table was used in the private dining room of the last **Windsor Castle**, during its period of service.*

patrons were Lord Roberts, Cecil John Rhodes and Rudyard Kipling.

To coincide with the visit of the Prince of Wales the majestic pillars at the entrance to the hotel's magnificent driveway were built in 1925. All the way up the long driveway are planted sixty Canary palms.

Interestingly, the pillars were nearly removed in 1975 by the Cape Town City Council as they were obstructing the widening of Orange Street. However, the public outcry was such that the Council decided to widen the road only as far as the pillars.

In more recent times guests have included Sir Arthur 'Bomber' Harris, Chief of Royal Air Force Bomber Command from 1942-45, Harold Macmillan, Edward Heath, Henry Kissinger, Sir Laurens van der Post (who thought it "the best hotel in the world"), Prince Philip, and entertainers, David Bowie, and John Lennon (under a false name).

If it is afternoon tea in style that you seek, there is but one place in Cape Town — the much loved "Nellie", where the event is memorable, its tradition being maintained, as one travel writer put it, "as if its guests were still off the Union-Castle steamer from the mother country." You may either partake *al fresco* on the terrace or in the main drawing room, where everything imag-

inable is laid out on a large mahogany dining table rescued by Union-Castle chairman Lord Cayzer from the private dining room of RMS *Windsor Castle* before she was sold on cessation of the mail service.

Many an anecdote is related about the legendary hotel. The late Dennis Morris recounted one of the most charming in his wine column in *The Daily Telegraph* following his visit to the Cape Winelands as one of the party I escorted there in 1975. He told of the two elderly sisters who, daily in the hotel's lounge, at the boom of Cape Town' midday gun, raised glasses of sparkling Nederburg Brut with the toast: "To dear Daddy, who made all this possible." To his delight Morris was contacted by one of the ladies who confirmed it was true. Of course it was! The "Nellie's" like that.

Nestling in the shadows of Cape Town's illustrious Table Mountain was the *Helmsley*. A former settler's home of around 1825, the modest two-star hotel had a charm of its own and was also owned by Union-Castle. It is now part of the *Mount Nelson*. During his visits to South Africa, Lord Cayzer, although staying at the "Nellie", frequently dined al fresco in the small garden of the Helmsley. One of its attractions for him was that over the years it had become a veritable Aladdin's cave of Union-Caste memorabilia and boasted many a rare photograph, poster or large oil painting of famous mailships that were so much a part of Cape Town life.

One Shrove Tuesday he was offered pancakes, which he accepted with pleasure. Returning to the *Mount Nelson*, the chairman asked to see the dinner menu and then sent for the manager. "Do you know which day it is," asked Lord Cayzer. The man, somewhat surprised, said: "Tuesday, sir." "Yes, but what Tuesday?" persisted the chairman. The poor man responded with the date. "No, no," said Cayzer, "It's Shrove Tuesday. Why weren't pancakes on the menu?"

## 1985

By now *Astor* was programmed to spend only half the year on the Golden Run. The remainder of her time being spent cruising in the Indian Ocean and to South America and the Antarctic.

In April came the news that *Astor* was to be sold. The reason for her withdrawal included the fact that she was not ideally suited for the South African route. The vessel was, after all, designed for short-sea cruising and to make her more flexible would have involved considerable conversion work.

In 1985 four members of the Palestinian Liberation Organisation hijacked *Achille Lauro* off Egypt, taking the four hundred passengers hostage in return for the release of fifty Palestinians from Israeli jails. After four days the gunman gave themselves up to the Egyptian authorities in return for safe passage. During their time on

**Achille Lauro**

board the terrorists shot sixty-year-old Leon Klinghoffer, a disabled American tourist in a wheelchair. They then pushed him overboard.

## 1986

*Astor* was duly sold and continued to sail under the name of *Arkona*, chartered to TVI of Germany. Simultaneously with the sale of *Astor* Safmarine announced they had com-

**Astor II,** *a virtual replica of* **Astor I,** *never made the Cape Run, concentrating instead on worldwide cruises.*

missioned the building in Kiel of a bigger *Astor* – 21 990 grt. She was to carry some 650 passengers, have more fuel-efficient engines, and to be some twelve metres longer, thereby fitting the average wave pattern and so ensuring smoother sailing.

There was a one-year gap while *Astor II* was built. Once delivered, she began cruising worldwide, being time chartered to Island Blythe with Morgan Leisure of Colchester as operators. They ran her until the end of 1988 when she was sold to Black Sea Shipping and operated under the name *Fedor Dostoevski* with a charter to Neckermann of Germany.

It is sad to reflect that all the excitement and enthusiasm generated at the special luncheon held at Southampton on board *Astor* on 3 April 1984 to celebrate the inaugural voyage to the Cape the next day, had in four years come to nothing.

All this time *RMS St Helena* was continuing to operate her regular service to and from South Africa. By the mid-1980s a replacement for her was being considered by the British Government. She was by then over twenty years old and had been running almost non-stop for more than a decade, added to which her seventy-six berths could, said the company, have been sold many times over each voyage.

## 1989

Eventually agreement was reached and a new RMS was launched on 31 October by HRH Prince Andrew, so renewing the Falklands link. The first combined cargo/passenger ship to be specially designed (by Three Quays Marine Services, London) and built by A& P Appledore (Aberdeen) Ltd to serve the island colony, she has grt of 6 767 and carries 128 passengers. With a length of 105 m and breath of 19,2 m, she has a speed of 15 knots.

While the new vessel – subsequently to be named *St Helena* – was being fitted out, the original renamed *St Helena Island* continued the 'Golden Run', finally docking at Avonmouth in late August 1990. She was then sold to Sea Safaris Ltd, Malta, re-registered at Valleta, and re-named, yet again, this time as *Avalon*. Plans to cruise her in the Indian Ocean failed to materialise and she was laid up in Durban, waiting to be sold.◆

## CHAPTER ELEVEN

# CRUISING INTO THE MILLENNIUM: 1990 – 2004

*The 53.050 grt. SA Winterberg, built in France in 1979, is one of four SAFmarine container ships sailing about every nine days from Tilbury to Cape Town with accommodation for ten passengers.*

### 1990

An announcement by Safmarine in Cape Town on 2 March 1990 heralded the company's return to a regular passenger service on the 'Golden Run' – albeit in limited form. From mid-May five double cabins were made available in four of their big white container ships serving Europe.

Built in France in the late 1970s and each of 53 000 grt plus, *SA Helderberg*, *SA Sederberg*, *SA Waterberg* and *SA Winterberg* operated out of Southampton every nine or so days for a fourteen day voyage to Cape Town, returning via the same West Coast route. With a regular link between the UK and South Africa re-established, the service proved an instant success and bookings remained very healthy, according to Safmarine.

The Swiss-based operator Mediterranean Shipping Company (MSC) has its UK base in Felixstowe from where its fleet of over forty vessels runs services worldwide. MSC first started a South African service in 1979 and seven main vessels operated a weekly service from Felixstowe (every Thursday) to Cape Town and Durban. Some of these ships carried twelve passengers, while others took only seven or eight. The company stated they were 'only too pleased to take passengers', but stressed this was not the main function of the service. A new venture for MSC in 1990 was the acquisition of Lauro Lines and, thereby *Achille Lauro* and the 21 000 grt ss Monterey.

### 1991

It was just like old times at Cape Town Docks in March 1991 as some of the top luxury liners prepared to set sail for Southampton and Tilbury. Once again, war was to play a part in the saga of the 'Golden Run.'

With the Middle East a no-go area, as a result of the Gulf War, world cruisers scheduled to return from Australia via the Suez Canal had to be rerouted to the Cape of Good Hope to make for home via the West Coast of Africa.

Two of the world's most famous ships – Cunard's 69 053 grt *Queen Elizabeth II* and P & O's 45 000 grt flagship *Canberra* – were moored in Table Bay prior to sailing to Southampton. They were joined by the 15 065 grt Russian ship *Azerbaijan* on charter to the British company CTC and *Achille Lauro*, finishing yet another of her voyages to and from South Africa. *Azerbaijan* was the first Russian liner to arrive in a South African port for thirty years and received a tremendous welcome.

*The Daily Telegraph* offered its readers in 1991 the opportunity of sailing to Cape Town. In attractive full page full colour advertisements the voyage was described as 'most unusual' and 'in depth.' Indeed, 'unique' would not have been an unreasonable description, for this was no line voyage but a cruise – and a most leisurely one at that, for the thirty-six day voyage took in no less than fifteen ports of call.

Sailing from Gibraltar on 26 October 1991, the 3 095 grt *MS Caledonian Star* called at the Atlantic islands of Madeira, Las Palmas, Gomera, Tenerife and Lanzarote before proceeding down Africa's west coast. Calls were then made at Dakar, Banjul (Gambia), Freetown, Abidjan (Ivory Coast), Tema, Accra (Ghana), Lorne (Togo), Sao Tome Island, Port Gentil (Gabon) and Matadi (Zaire). After two calls at Namibia – Walvis Bay and Port Nolloth – the vessel finally docked at Cape Town on 30 November.

There were no plans to repeat this odyssey, but its unusual itinerary did highlight the great variety of ports of call available to operators planning cruises on the traditional Golden Run.

## 1992

From 1992 P&O World Cruises were to include the Cape in their itineraries. On 10 January, the 28 000 grt *Sea Princess* left Southampton for Cape Town via Tenerife, Dakar and Abidjan and thence to the Far East and USA. In March *Canberra* again called at Cape Town on her way home to Southampton from Australia and the Far East, a voyage that was to be repeated in March 1993.

Not surprisingly, port facilities at Cape Town were experiencing a boom. In 1991 services were twenty-four per cent up on the previous year and the volume of exports and imports substantially increased. Ocean liners, tankers and many other vessels made good use of the dry-dock facilities, and the repair yards were fully utilised.

Following her return to Southampton on 13 June from yet another voyage to and from South Africa, that grand old lady of the sea *Achille Lauro* spent summer cruising to Greece and Turkey. A month prior to her arrival home SAGA, who specialises in holidays tailored for travellers aged fifty-plus, announced 'an exciting and great value opportunity to cruise to Cape Town this winter.'

On 22 November the *Blue Lady*, as she was affectionately known, left Southampton to sail outwards via the West Coast. *Achille Lauro* docked in Cape Town on 9 December, returning eventually to the UK by way of the East Coast and Suez.

Also in November of that year Italy's foremost cruiser line, Costa, sent the 16 495 grt *Enrico Costa* around Africa. Leaving Genoa on 15 November she sailed out via Suez, with calls at the Seychelles and Madagascar, to Durban and Cape Town, returning to Southampton via the West Coast route with stopovers at Las Palmas and Lisbon. In 1990 *Enrico Costa* had undergone major refurbishments, including the fittings of new engines. She carried a maximum of eight hundred passengers.

**Kareliya**

## 1993

No doubt heartened by the great reception afforded *Azerbaijan* when she docked in Cape Town in March 1991, CTC Cruise Lines announced in April 1992 that her sister ship the line's flagship *Kareliya* (15 000 grt) would be making a grand cruise around Africa early in the New Year. She was scheduled to sail from Tilbury on 6 January 1993 to the Cape on what the line nostalgically called 'the old UK/Cape Town mail run.' Built in Finland in 1976 and extensively refurbished in 1989 *Kareliya* was British-managed, crewed by Russians and carried some five hundred passengers. The twenty-one night voyage to Cape Town included calls at Lisbon, Las Palmas, Gambia, Togo, and Walvis Bay, after which the homeward voyage would be via the East Coast and Suez.

Formed in 1966 CTC (Charter Travel Club) initially operated voyages between UK and Australia to serve the family reunion market. Then in the mid-seventies, responding to market changes, CTC started to concentrate on cruising.

The establishment of the Ukraine as a newly independent state resulted in CTC dropping the old Soviet hammer and sickle insignia from the funnels of the former USSR passenger fleet. This was replaced by a new design incorporating the Ukrainian colours

*Captain Severov welcomes Linda aboard the Kareliya.*

97

**Kareliya** *at Lisbon.*

and showing a yellow roundel centred on a powder-blue band, which featured a black, stylised trident, a traditional national and religious symbol. *Kareliya* commenced her 1993 cruising season displaying the new livery.

Keen to obtain more details of the January voyage, I called at CTC's office in London and saw their passenger services manager, Andy Whitehouse. Expressing the reason for my interest – Union-Castle – Andy quickly revealed he had served with

**Belein Tower, Lisbon.**

the company as third purser on *Pendennis Castle*, *SA Vaal* and finally on the last voyage of the *Windsor Castle*. He had also acted as cruise director on the *Astor*.

The net result was Linda and I were set to sail on *Kareliya* with me giving talks and tastings of Cape wines and a course of talks on the Golden Run.

We duly sailed from Tilbury (which now boasted the title of London International Cruise Terminal) at 5 pm on Wednesday 6 January. It would not be unfair to say that many of the more elderly passengers faced with some apprehension the thousand mile haul through the British Channel and the Bay of Biscay to our first port of call, Lisbon. In the event they need not have worried, as despite a certain amount of rolling in the Channel, the Bay was uncharacteristically docile. The West African ports of call were fascinating, particularly Gambia where we were at anchor for two days.

Four talks, followed by showing of a film, were carried out in the ship's cinema, with the tastings in the adjoining minor bar.

*Monument to the Discoveries, Lisbon.*

They proved extremely popular, so that those wishing to attend had to register at the Information Office between 10 and 11 am on the morning of each tasting, attendance being restricted to the one hundred and twenty person capacity of the cinema. Usually by five minutes to ten some two dozen were waiting to register.

All in all, it was a delightful voyage. I had the opportunity of a chat with the ship's master, Captain Stanislav Severov, who told me he thought the four hundred passengers plus the ideal complement as it enabled each of them to 'receive full and proper attention', added to which 'it facilitated shore excursion arrangements.' Will *Kareliya* make the Cape Town run again? I asked him. He thought so. She did, the next year.

As I left the Captain's cabin, Captain Severov gave me a handsome brochure containing full details of the BLASCO (Black Sea Shipping Company) passenger fleet. On the page devoted to *MS Fedor Dostoyevski* – and beneath a colour photograph of the vessel in the overall details appeared the note: "Built Kiel 1986 – ex *Astor*."

All the ship's officers and crew were Ukrainian. Of the dozen top executive officers one was a woman – chief purser Galina Shabarina. She amused us in the ship's concert by telling a string of risqué stories in very bad English. Our cabin stewardess Nadja had more than a smattering of English and kept our cabin immaculate. They all contributed to a delightful voyage.

Returning to the Cape wine tastings, thirty bottles remained over at the end of the four tastings and it was arranged with the cruise director Peter Warren that they be raffled with the proceeds going to the Odessa Children's Home Fund. A total of £181 was collected and ten prizes of three bottles each were drawn for later that day in the music salon in front of a large audience. That event, held just prior to our reaching Cape Town, underlined just how happy a voyage it had been.

Later that year, Linda and I were delighted to be invited to CTC's 1992 Travel Trade Awards Luncheon held on board *Kareliya* at Tilbury on 6 April, and to meet again so soon Captain Severov, some of his officers, our fellow lecturers and of course, Andy Whitehouse, who had sailed with us

*Statue of Henry the Navigator.*

**Black Watch**

as far as Lisbon. The awards were presented by the gorgeous and so sadly missed Jill Dando on her BBC's *Holiday '93* programme.

By now Safmarine had decided to move the UK side of their operation from Southampton to Tilbury because of the serious congestion developing at the Hampshire docks. In addition, the London port was, said the company, more cost-effective and a better distribution point. Similarly, Curnow Shipping found a move from Avonmouth to Cardiff as St Helena's port of departure financially advantageous.

## 1994

Despite many setbacks – a fire in the cinema, impounded for a year in Tenerife; and of course, the horrific hi-jacking – *Achille Lauro* had proved a popular ship on the South and East African run. The final disaster befell her in November 1994 en route to Cape Town when she caught fire off the African coast. She was abandoned and sank two days later.

## 1995

By now the availability of sailings to South Africa and, indeed, types of voyages, had seldom been more varied, such opportunities offering even more choice for the discerning traveller to sail south to the sun on the historic 'Golden Run.'

## 1996

Fred Olsen Cruises, which as a family operation, had had a long history of cruising, purchased the 28 492 grt *Black Watch* from the Norwegian Cruise Line and arranged a refitting programme. At the last minute the previous owners decided to take up an option to extend its charter by a month with the result that the refitting was delayed.

The inaugural long-haul voyage was planned to leave Dover on Saturday 4 January 1997 for Cape Town via Tenerife, Mindelo (Cape Verde Islands), St Helena and Walvis Bay. Prior to this there was to be a debut voyage – a shakedown cruise, but with passengers – in the Mediterranean.

**Black Watch** *at Tenerife.*

*Odessa Childrens' Home fundraising.*

It had been four years since that fun voyage aboard the Ukrainian ship *Kareliya*, so when I learned in the spring of 1996 of the planned *Black Watch* cruise to the Cape, I wrote to Fred Olsen Cruises, offering my services as guest lecturer. At the end of June I received a charming letter from Lorraine Dymoke White, the fleet product manager, saying she was "delighted, that accompanied by my wife, I would be able to join *Black Watch* as guest lecturer." Olsens were also agreeable to Cape wines being added to the ship's wine list, in addition to those earmarked for my tastings.

## 1997

On Friday 3 January I had a phone call from Lorraine to say that the *Black Watch* had hit heavy weather in the Bay of Biscay on return from her debut voyage. This had slowed her down and would delay our sailing the next day. We were therefore not required to be at the Dover Cruise Terminal until Saturday evening.

We drove down in a snowstorm and on arrival at the dockside were surprised to find passengers were only just disembarking. The embarkation time was announced as 10.30 pm, but we did not in fact go on board until 11.30 pm. On awakening the next morning we found to our amazement we were still in dock and eventually sailed at 10.15 am.

The next day I thought I had better check my wine stocks and found to my horror that only forty of the total one hundred and fifty cases had been loaded on board by the time we sailed. The wine I had available

consisted of twenty cases of white wine and twenty of sparkling. With the agreement of cruise director Derek Mann and the *maitre'd* it was arranged that I give my talk on Cape wines, followed by a winelands film, finishing up by announcing that bottles of the white wine would be on every table at dinner that night, and a similar arrangement would be made the night before we docked at Cape Town. Happily, this was well-received.

At 4 am on Tuesday 7 January, the Bay started doing its worst and this continued well into the morning. It was revealed later by the Captain that it had been Storm strength 11, which reduced the ship's speed to 11 knots an hour, and by 1 pm it was Gale strength 8.

Two of the day's lecturers had fallen by the wayside and Derek Mann asked if I would be prepared to bring my *Every Thursday at four o'clock* talk forward to that afternoon. "You'll be lucky," he said, "if you get half a dozen in the audience!" How wrong he was. The Marina Theatre's capacity was two hundred, but it was a full house with many sitting in the aisles. The question and answer session went on for fifty minutes, confirming the great interest there was – and still is – in the Union-Castle Line and the 'Golden Run.'

*Black Watch* proved a comfortable and well-run ship with many attractive features, such as the Observatory Bar where one enjoyed a panoramic view of the way ahead. The one disappointment was that we were unable to go ashore at St Helena, the local authorities saying it was too rough for us to land. All in all, a most enjoyable voyage, and one that the *Black Watch* has repeated since on several occasions.

*Newspaper advert for Union-Castle's Centenary.*

**Newspaper advert for Union-Castle's Centenary.**

**Caronia**

Caronia

## 1998 / 1999

Cruising was by then a fast expanding sector of the leisure market. Faith in its future was marked by the building of ever new tonnage, while the decision at this time by P&O to 'go back to its roots' and concentrate on the booming trade in cruise holidays were further evidence of this.

One organisation which joined those sailing the 'Golden Run' was SAGA's shipping subsidiary with the beautiful 24 474 grt *Saga Rose*, which has since graced the South African ports on many occasions.

## 2000

Had it survived ever-increasing costs, competition from the airlines and freight containerisation, the once mighty Union-Castle Mail Steamship Co Ltd would have been celebrating its centenary this year. Happily, the occasion did not pass unnoticed. Thanks to the imagination and initiative of a former Union-Castle skipper, Captain Richard Hollyer, the great name was resurrected and the historic passenger service to the Cape relaunched in December 1999 – for one voyage only – to mark both the Line's one hundredth birthday and the Millennium. As early as February 1999 advertisements were appearing in the national press, announcing 'the relaunch of a legend' and 'celebrate the Millennium Union-Castle style.'

Sadly, in April of that year Lord Cayzer died. It was as Sir Nicholas that he ran the company from 1958 to 1977. One of his last acts was to give his fullest personal support to the special voyage. In the magnificent brochure produced to publicise this exciting venture, he wrote that he was delighted to offer his personal support. He would, I am sure, have loved to have joined the sailing, but he will be remembered as one of the leading figures of the post-war shipping industry.

For this commemorative voyage the 28 000 grt *MV Victoria* was chartered from P & O, as it was felt that her lines were closest to those of the memorable Union-Castle mailships.

The sixty-six night gala cruise around Africa started from Southampton at 1 pm on 11 December 1999, sailing south to Cape Town via Madeira, Las Palmas, Dakar, St Helena (with Christmas at sea, before reaching Walvis Bay). Over the millennium period *Victoria* was moored alongside the Victoria & Alfred Waterfront, Cape Town, where passengers watched the city's spectacular New Year's Eve fireworks display. They left Cape Town on

**MV Victoria**

2 January 2000 to proceed up the coast of East Africa and thence via Suez and the Mediterranean, finally docking in Southampton on 15 February.

Surely conscious of the occasion, Cunard announced that their 20 000 grt *Caronia* (the former *Vistafjord*) was to 'create the Cape Town Line voyages.' A subsequent advertisement read: "Cunard launch a grand British tradition – long, leisurely line voyages to South Africa. For those who missed cruising's first Golden Age, Cunard has recreated the legendary line voyages. Now you too can experience the relaxed luxury of a great sea voyage to and from Cape Town." A 'line voyage' is a system of regular sea travel over a definite route, whereas a cruise is a sea voyage solely for pleasure stopping at various ports.

*Caronia* sailed from Southampton on 11 January, calling at Madeira, Cape Verde Islands, and Ascension and docking in Cape Town on 28 January, returning on the same route, but substituting the call at Ascension for one at St Helena.

Cunard's connection with Union-Castle goes back a long way. Sir Donald Currie, chairman of the Castle Line, which merged with the Union Line in 1900, painted the new ships' funnels bright red with black topping, as a compliment to his early employers, Cunard. As a charming gesture P&O had *Victoria's* funnel repainted red and black.

Still today, the name Union-Castle arouses great interest and enthusiasm among many people who inevitably ask, "Whatever happened to those beautiful ships with their graceful lines?"

## 2001

On 15 February 2001 the P&O's *MV Victoria* successfully masquerading as a Union-Castle Line mailship, docked in Southampton. It is at this stage that I finish my story.◆

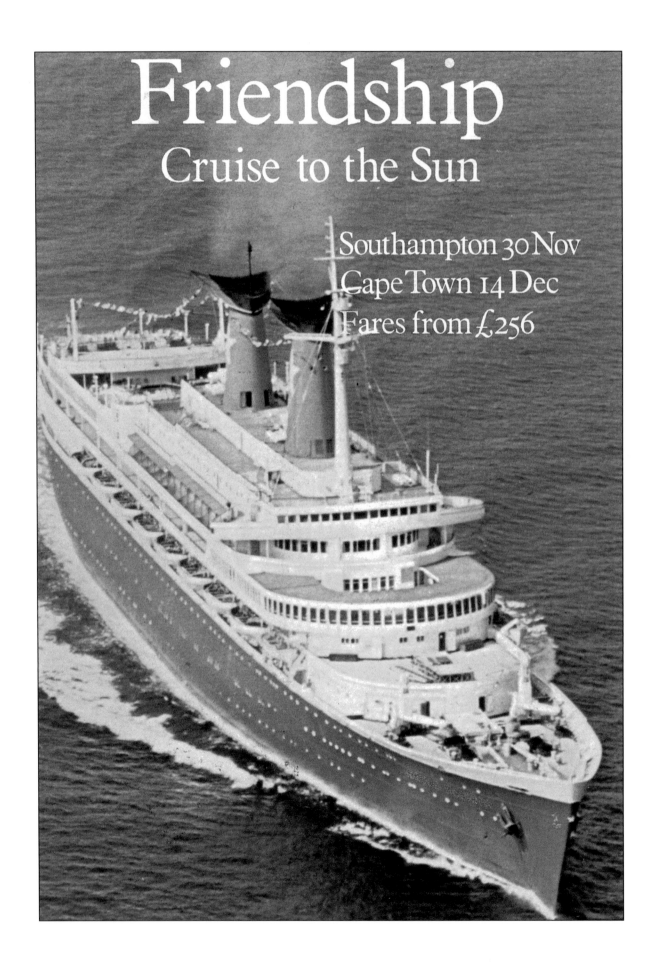

# Friendship
## Cruise to the Sun

Southampton 30 Nov
Cape Town 14 Dec
Fares from £256

## CONCLUSION

# THE END OF AN ERA

The autumn of 2004 was to see the end of regular passenger line services from the United Kingdom to the Cape. For close on two hundred years the service represented a remarkable chapter in maritime history. Early in 2004 Safmarine announced that it was to cease operating on the Golden Run.

So it was that when on 30 October 2004 the *SA Winterberg* from Europe docked in Cape Town it was the final such voyage by Safmarine. For the previous fourteen years Safmarine had offered accommodation for up to twelve passengers on a number of their working cargo container ships. Each month there were approximately two voyages either southbound from Tilbury, or north to the United Kingdom form Cape Town. The service had proved popular with those wishing 'to get away from it all' as life on board provided complete relaxation and a pressure-free lifestyle.

Twenty-four days earlier – on 6 October 2004 – the *St Helena* docked in Cape Town, having left the United Kingdom for the last time on 7 September to make Cape Town her new home port. From Cape Town she will operate a regular service to Ascension Island via Luderitz, Walvis Bay and St Helena and back again to South Africa. Interestingly in 1966 the Capetown Castle ran an extra sixteen day service to Southampton to the Cape by way of Madeira, Ascension, St Helena and Walvis Bay.

In addition, the RAF at Brize Norton in Oxfordshire can now fly passengers to Ascension Island and return so that one can still sail from Ascension to Cape Town and back.

The Royal mailship *St Helena* is one of six members of the rather exclusive Niche Cruise Alliance, which describes itself as 'A collection of diverse cruise experiences.' Other members include Orient-Express, whose hotel division own the *Mount Nelson Hotel*, Cape Town, and *Reid's Palace Hotel*, both with strong Union-Castle connections.

So ends the saga of the legendary Cape Run – The Golden Run. The major player was Union-Castle who, following the merger in 1900 of the Union and Castle Lines, for the next seventy seven years sailed each and every week with unfailing regularity 'south to the sun of South Africa.' Other important contributors to the mail service were Safmarine and St Helena Line.

Originally established in 1946, Safmarine had close connections with Union-Castle, with which she shared the mail run from 1968 to 1977. Safmarine will also be remembered for their gallant efforts to re-establish the historic run in 1984 with the beautiful cruise ship *Astor*.

Last but certainly not least, is the vital role played by the St Helena Line in maintaining contact on a regular basis with both Ascension and St Helena Islands from the cessation of Union-Castle voyages until her new role in 2004.

In May 2004, twenty-seven years after the company's closure, a 'Grand Reunion' was held at a Southampton hotel. Of the two hundred and fifty invited only sixty-five did not attend and of the one hundred and eighty-five present, some had come on journeys two or three hours away which epitomise the deep affection in which Union-Castle is still held and, indeed, how very special it is to those who worked for the line.◆

CABIN DE LUXE      FIRST CLASS CABIN

In the 'Pendennis Castle' the eight de luxe cabins and both the suites are air-conditioned. Four of the de luxe cabins can be turned into sitting rooms. All other cabins have punka louvre ventilation. A Children's Nursery, with constant and kindly supervision, allows parents to relax in peace.

FIRST CLASS PLAYROOM      SUITE BEDROOM

**Pendennis Castle** *cabin accommodation.*

## EPILOGUE

Historically the Golden Run is over five hundred years old, for it was in the year 1488 that the Portuguese mariner Bartholomew Dias rounded the Cape of Good Hope. From 1394 to his death in 1460 Prince Henry the Navigator, infante of Portugal, devoted his energies to the encouragement of exploration and before he died, his sailors had reconnoitered the West Coast of Africa as far as Sierra Leone. On ascending to the throne John II, King of Portugal, resumed the discovery of the African coast.

As we have seen, the Bay of Biscay caused more trouble than that to *World Renaissance* and *Astor* in their attempts to restart a regular service to the Cape. Neither vessel was really suited to the rigors of the Atlantic. The Union-Castle mailships had the advantage that they invariably carried large amounts of cargo, and therefore sat solidly in the water. Indeed, the first mailship to be filled with stabilisers was *Pendennis Castle* (1959).

Decisions not to cross the Bay "for the safety and comfort of passengers and crew" necessitated in sailing from and docking at Lisbon, somewhat appropriate historically. Appropriate in that it was from Lisbon that those intrepid Portuguese mariners set sail on their voyages of discovery.

Starting our voyage of discovery from Lisbon enabled us to visit the Maritime Museum, where in the main entrance hall, is a large and impressive state of Henry the Navigator. Outside, nearby, is the lavishly decorated Belem Tower, from where the explorers were given a rousing send-off, while on the other side of the Tagus estuary is the famous monument to the Discoveries, built to commemorate the 500th anniversary of the death of Prince Henry.

Today with tourism to South Africa in general, and the Cape in particular booming, and an availability of sailing on the Golden Run as never before, the future is now set fair for the Fairest Cape.

I consider myself so fortunate in having played a small, but rewarding part in the history of the Union-Castle Line and of The Golden Run – I hope you have enjoyed reading about it.◆